BAPTIST CONFESSION *of*

FAITH

& CATECHISM

for DISPENSATIONAL CHURCHES

"For years I have described myself as a confessionalist, in principle, in a theological community that by-and-large does not value shared confessions. I am encouraged that this project is addressing that deficiency and am hopeful that it will bring dispensational Baptists closer to the realization of confessional unity."

MARK SNOEBERGER

Professor of Systematic Theology and Apologetics

Detroit Baptist Theological Seminary, Allen Park, MI

"An unfortunate tendency of popular dispensationalism has been a disdain for church history and for creeds and confessions in particular. The unique authority of Scripture has been warped into a disregard for the work of 'the shepherds and teachers,' gifts to the church from our risen Lord. As dispensationalists, we have Scripture-driven commitments that distinguish us from our other Reformed brothers, and we should make those differences clear. But we still hold much in common with them and we should rejoice to affirm those shared doctrines. I am delighted to see the publication of this confession as a step to accomplish both of these worthy ambitions."

MICHAEL RILEY

Pastor, Calvary Baptist Church, Wakefield, MI

THE

Baptist Confession *of*

FAITH

& Catechism

for Dispensational Churches

BRANDON JAMES CRAWFORD

Ambassador International
GREENVILLE, SOUTH CAROLINA & BELFAST, NORTHERN IRELAND

www.ambassador-international.com

The Baptist Confession of Faith and Catechism for Dispensational Churches

©2023 by Brandon James Crawford
All rights reserved

Hardcover ISBN: 978-1-64960-489-7
Paperback ISBN: 978-1-64960-387-6
eISBN: 978-1-64960-389-0

Cover Design by Hannah Linder Designs
Interior Design by Dentelle Design
Edited by Katie Cruice Smith

Scripture quotations are from the ESV® Bible (The Holy Bible, English Standard Version®), copyright © 2001 by Crossway, a publishing ministry of Good News Publishers. Used by permission. All rights reserved. The ESV text may not be quoted in any publication made available to the public by a Creative Commons license. The ESV may not be translated in whole or in part into any other language.

No part of this publication may be reproduced, distributed, or transmitted in any form or by any means, including photocopying, recording, or other electronic or mechanical methods, without the prior written permission of the publisher, except in the case of brief quotations embodied in critical reviews and certain other noncommercial uses permitted by copyright law. For permission requests, contact the publisher using the information below.

AMBASSADOR INTERNATIONAL
Emerald House Group, Inc.
411 University Ridge, Suite B14
Greenville, SC 29601
United States
www.ambassador-international.com

AMBASSADOR BOOKS
The Mount
2 Woodstock Link
Belfast, BT6 8DD
Northern Ireland, United Kingdom
www.ambassadormedia.co.uk

The colophon is a trademark of Ambassador, a Christian publishing company.

CONTENTS

FOREWORD

The author of Hebrews laid upon churches the solemn responsibility, "Remember your leaders, those who spoke to you the word of God . . . imitate their faith" (13:7 ESV). We "remember" those who have gone before us when we value and perpetuate the doctrinal legacy they bequeathed to succeeding generations. The seventeenth century Baptists who stood up for truth as part of the English Separatist movement, and expressed that truth in The Baptist Confession of 1689, left a legacy worthy to be remembered and imitated. Their heirs suffered and served to advance the cause of Jesus Christ in the centuries that followed. Unfortunately, the value of historic confessions of faith and catechisms has been largely lost in the current generation of Christians. Overlooking the importance of history, many dismiss the idea of a confession of faith as arcane and limiting. Others prefer a "roll your own" approach, each man or church crafting a personal, unique confession.

Brandon Crawford has done a great service for Baptist churches that stand for historic theology and embrace a dispensational hermeneutic. His "gentle" revision of these works upholds the faith of our fathers in the same spirit that moved them to build on the works of others; he shows "no itch to clog religion with new words," but simply uses "that form of sound words which hath been, in consent with the Holy Scriptures, used by others before us." The result is a set of tools that will enable churches effectively to demonstrate their role as the nexus between past and future, uphold the proper catholicity of the faith, and stand against contemporary conceit that equates wisdom with originality. My prayer is that this work will become widely known and widely used.

STEVEN THOMAS

Pastor, Huron Baptist Church, Flat Rock, MI

INTRODUCTION TO
THE BAPTIST CONFESSION OF FAITH

In 1677, Baptist pastors Nehemiah Coxe and William Collins drew up a confession of faith for the Petty France Church in London. The confession was approved by the congregation and then distributed to other Baptist churches in Great Britain, where it was enthusiastically embraced. Twelve years later, in 1689, representatives of more than one hundred Baptist churches meeting in general assembly formally adopted the second edition as their doctrinal standard.

The Baptist Confession of Faith (also known as the *Second London Baptist Confession*) has since become the most important summary of Baptist teachings in the English-speaking world. Not long after its adoption in Great Britain, it crossed the Atlantic and became the standard for Baptist churches throughout the American colonies. In the North, it was called the *Philadelphia Confession,* and in the South, the *Charleston Confession.* Today, it is used by Baptist churches all over the world.

The authors drew most of the language for *The Baptist Confession* directly from the *Westminster Confession* of the Presbyterians, with some supplemental material coming from the *Savoy Declaration* of the Congregationalists. In places where the authors needed to outline Baptist distinctives, their wording was original.

The Baptist Confession is more than just a statement of faith. It is a fully orbed system of doctrine that has stood the test of time. This new edition retains the timeless language of the original with just a few minor alterations to make it compatible with dispensationalism. It is my conviction that dispensational theology has been a largely positive development within the Reformed tradition. Its greatest contribution has been the application of an originalist hermeneutic to all of Scripture, including its poetic and prophetic portions. The results have given us a clearer understanding of the relationship between the Old and New Covenants, the spirituality of the Church, and the doctrine of Last Things—thus the need for a gentle revision of this historic confession.

My hope for this new edition is that it will be used of God to ground thousands of individuals, families, and churches in biblical doctrine, that it will give them a better appreciation of their rich ecclesiastical heritage, and that it will equip them with wisdom for contemporary ministry.

"Be not ashamed of your faith," Charles Spurgeon once wrote. "Remember it is the ancient gospel of martyrs, confessors, reformers and saints. Above all, it is the truth of God, against which the gates of Hell cannot prevail."

Brandon Crawford
Marshall, Michigan
Reformation Day 2021

TO THE JUDICIOUS AND IMPARTIAL READER

Courteous Reader, it is now many years since divers of us (with other sober Christians then living and walking in the way of the Lord that we profess) did conceive ourselves to be under a necessity of publishing a Confession of our faith for the information and satisfaction of those who did not thoroughly understand what our principles were or who had entertained prejudices against our profession by reason of the strange representation of them by some men of note who had taken very wrong measures and, accordingly, led others into misapprehension of us and them. And this was first put forth about the year 1643 in the name of seven congregations then gathered in London, since which time divers' impressions thereof have been dispersed abroad and our end proposed in good measure answered, inasmuch as many (and some of those men eminent both for piety and learning) were thereby satisfied that we were no way guilty of those heterodoxies and fundamental errors which had too frequently been charged upon us without ground or occasion given on our part.

And forasmuch as that Confession is not now commonly to be had, and also that many others have since embraced the same truth which is owned therein, it was judged necessary by us to join together in giving a testimony to the world of our firm adherence to those wholesome principles by the publication of this which is now in your hand. And forasmuch as our method and manner of expressing our sentiments in this doth vary from the former (although the substance of this matter is the same), we shall freely impart to you the reason and occasion thereof. One thing that greatly prevailed with us to undertake this work was not only to give a full account of ourselves to those Christians who differ from us about the subject of baptism but also the profit that might from thence arise unto those who have any account of our labors in their instruction and establishment in the great truths of the Gospel in the clear understanding and steady belief of which our comfortable walking with God and fruitfulness before Him in all our ways is most nearly concerned; and therefore, we did conclude it necessary to express ourselves the more fully and distinctly; and also to fix on such a method as might be most comprehensive of those things we designed to explain our sense and belief of; and finding no defect in this regard in that fixed on by the Assembly, and, after them by those of the congregational way, we did readily conclude it best to retain the same order in our present Confession. And also, when we observed that those last mentioned did in their Confessions (for reasons which seemed of weight both to themselves and others) choose not only to express their mind in words concurrent with the former in sense concerning all those articles wherein they were agreed, but also, for the most part, without any variation of the terms, we did in like manner conclude it best to follow their example in making use of the very same words with them both in these articles (which are very many) wherein our faith and doctrine are the same with theirs; and this we did the more abundantly to manifest our consent with both in all the fundamental articles of the Christian religion, as also with many others whose orthodox Confessions have been published to the world on the behalf of the Protestant in diverse nations and cities. And also to convince all that we have no itch to clog religion with new words but do readily acquiesce in that form of sound words which hath been, in consent with the Holy Scriptures, used by others before us, hereby declaring, before God, angels, and men, our hearty agreement with them in that wholesome Protestant doctrine which, with so clear evidence of Scriptures, they have asserted. Some things, indeed, are in some places added, some terms omitted, and some few changed; but these alterations are of that nature as that we need not doubt any charge or suspicion of unsoundness in the faith from any of our brethren upon the account of them.

In those things wherein we differ from others, we have expressed ourselves with all candor and plainness that none might entertain jealousy of aught secretly lodged in our breasts that we would not want the world to be acquainted with; yet we hope we have also observed those rules of modesty and humility as will render our freedom in this respect inoffensive, even to those whose sentiments are different from ours.

We have also taken care to affix texts of Scripture at the bottom for the confirmation of each article in our Confession; in which work we have studiously endeavored to select such as are most clear and pertinent for the proof of what is asserted by us; and our earnest desire is that all into whose hands this may come would follow that (never enough commended) example of the noble Bereans, who searched the Scriptures daily that they might find out whether the things preached to them were so or not.

There is one thing more which we sincerely profess and earnestly desire credence in—viz., that contention is most remote from our design in all that we have done in this matter; and we hope that the liberty of an ingenuous unfolding of our principles and opening our hearts unto our brethren with the scriptural grounds of our faith and practice will by none of them be either denied to us or taken ill from us. Our whole design is accomplished if we may have attained that justice as to be measured in our principles and practice and the judgment of both by others, according to what we have now published, which the Lord (Whose eyes are as a flame of fire) knoweth to be the doctrine which with our hearts we most firmly believe and sincerely endeavor to conform our lives to. And O that, other contentions being laid asleep, the only care and contention of all upon whom the name of our blessed Redeemer is called might for the future be to walk humbly with their God in the exercise of all love and meekness toward each other, to perfect holiness in the fear of the Lord, each one endeavoring to have his conversation such as becometh the Gospel; and also, suitable to his place and capacity, vigorously to promote in others the practice of true religion and undefiled in the sight of God our Father! And that in this backsliding day, we might not spend our breath in fruitless complaints of the evils of others, but may everyone begin at home to reform in the first place our own hearts and ways, and then to quicken all that we may have influence upon to the same work, that if the will of God were so, none might deceive themselves by resting in and trusting in a form of godliness without the power of it, and inward experience of the efficacy of those truths that are professed by them.

And verily, there is one spring and cause of the decay of religion in our day which we cannot but touch upon and earnestly urge a redress of, and that is the neglect of the worship of God in families by those to whom the charge and conduct of them is committed. May not the gross ignorance and instability of many, with the profaneness of others, be justly charged upon their parents and masters, who have not trained them up in the way wherein they ought to walk when they were young, but have neglected those frequent and solemn commands which the Lord hath laid upon them, so to catechise and instruct them that their tender years might be seasoned with the knowledge of the truth of God as revealed in the Scriptures; and also by their own omission of prayer and other duties of religion of their families, together with the ill example of their loose conversation, having inured them first to a neglect of and the contempt of all piety and religion? We know this will not excuse the blindness and wickedness of any, but certainly it will fall heavily upon those who have been thus the occasion thereof; they indeed die in their sins, but will not their blood be required of those under whose care they were, who yet permitted them to go on without warning—yea, led them into the paths of destruction? And will not the diligence of Christians with respect to the discharge of these duties in ages past rise up in judgment against and condemn many of those who would be esteemed such now?

We shall conclude with our earnest prayer that the God of all grace will pour out those measures of His Holy Spirit upon us, that the profession of truth may be accompanied with the sound belief and diligent practice of it by us, that His name may in all things be glorified through Jesus Christ our Lord. Amen.

CHAPTER 1

THE HOLY SCRIPTURES

1. The Holy Scripture is the only sufficient, certain, and infallible rule of all saving knowledge, faith, and obedience;[1] although the light of nature and the works of creation and Providence do so far manifest the goodness, wisdom, and power of God as to leave men inexcusable, yet are they not sufficient to give that knowledge of God and His will which is necessary unto salvation.[2] Therefore, it pleased the Lord at sundry times and in divers manners to reveal Himself and to declare His will unto His people[3] and afterward, for the better preserving and propagating of the truth and for the more sure establishment and comfort of His people against the corruption of the flesh and the malice of Satan and of the world, to commit the same wholly unto writing, which makes the Holy Scriptures to be most necessary, those former ways of God's revealing His will unto His people being now ceased.[4]

---

1   2 Timothy 3:15-17; Isaiah 8:20; Luke 16:29, 31; Ephesians 2:20
2   Romans 1:19-21, 2:14-15; Psalm 19:1-3
3   Hebrews 1:1
4   Proverbs 22:19-21; Romans 15:4; 2 Peter 1:19-20

2. Under the name of Holy Scripture or the written Word of God are now contained all the books of the Old and New Testaments, which are these:

Of the Old Testament: Genesis, Exodus, Leviticus, Numbers, Deuteronomy, Joshua, Judges, Ruth, 1 Samuel, 2 Samuel, 1 Kings, 2 Kings, 1 Chronicles, 2 Chronicles, Ezra, Nehemiah, Esther, Job, Psalms, Proverbs, Ecclesiastes, the Song of Songs, Isaiah, Jeremiah, Lamentations, Ezekiel, Daniel, Hosea, Joel, Amos, Obadiah, Jonah, Micah, Nahum, Habakkuk, Zephaniah, Haggai, Zechariah, Malachi.

Of the New Testament: Matthew; Mark; Luke; John; the Acts of the Apostles; Paul's Epistle to the Romans; 1 Corinthians; 2 Corinthians; Galatians; Ephesians; Philippians; Colossians; 1 Thessalonians; 2 Thessalonians; 1 Timothy; 2 Timothy; Titus; Philemon; the Epistle to the Hebrews; the Epistle of James; the first and second Epistles of Peter; the first, second, and third Epistles of John; the Epistle of Jude; the Revelation.

All which are given by the inspiration of God to be the rule of faith and life.[5]

3. The books commonly called Apocrypha, not being of Divine inspiration, are no part of the canon or rule of the Scripture and therefore are of no authority to the Church of God nor to be any otherwise approved or made use of than other human writings.[6]

---

5   2 Timothy 3:16
6   Luke 24:27, 44; Romans 3:2

4. The authority of the Holy Scripture, for which it ought to be believed, depends not upon the testimony of any man or church, but wholly upon God Who is Truth itself, the Author thereof; therefore, it is to be received because it is the Word of God.[7]

5. We may be moved and induced by the testimony of the Church of God to a high and reverent esteem of the Holy Scriptures; and the heavenliness of the matter, the efficacy of the doctrine, and the majesty of the style, the consent of all the parts, the scope of the whole which is to give all glory to God, the full discovery it makes of the only way of man's salvation, and many other incomparable excellencies and entire perfections thereof are arguments whereby it doth abundantly evidence itself to be the Word of God; yet notwithstanding, our full persuasion and assurance of the infallible truth and Divine authority thereof is from the inward work of the Holy Spirit, bearing witness by and with the word in our hearts.[8]

6. The whole counsel of God concerning all things necessary for His own glory, man's salvation, faith, and life is either expressly set down or necessarily contained in the Holy Scripture, unto which nothing at any time is to be added, whether by new revelation of the Spirit or traditions of men.[9]

---

7   2 Peter 1:19-21; 2 Timothy 3:16; 2 Thessalonians 2:13; 1 John 5:9
8   John 16:13-14; 1 Corinthians 2:10-12; 1 John 2:20
9   2 Timothy 3:15-17; Galatians 1:8-9

Nevertheless, we acknowledge the inward illumination of the Spirit of God to be necessary for the saving understanding of such things as are revealed in the Word[10] and that there are some circumstances concerning the worship of God and governance of the Church common to human actions and societies which are to be ordered by the light of nature and Christian prudence according to the general rules of the Word, which are always to be observed.[11]

7. All things in Scripture are not alike plain in themselves nor alike clear unto all;[12] yet those things which are necessary to be known, believed, and observed for salvation are so clearly propounded and opened in some place of Scripture or other that not only the learned, but also the unlearned, in a due use of ordinary means, may attain to a sufficient understanding of them.[13]

8. The Old Testament in Hebrew, which was the native language of the people of God of old,[14] and the New Testament in Greek, which at the time of the writing of it was most generally known to the nations, being immediately inspired by God, and by His singular care and Providence kept pure in all ages, are therefore authentic,[15] so as in all controversies

---

10   John 6:45; 1 Corinthians 2:9,10,11,12
11   1 Corinthians 11:13-14; 14:26, 40
12   2 Peter 3:16
13   Psalm 19:7; 119:130
14   Romans 3:2
15   Isaiah 8:20

of religion, the Church is finally to appeal unto them. But because these original tongues are not known to all the people of God,[16] who have a right unto and interest in the Scriptures and are commanded in the fear of God to read and search them,[17] therefore, they are to be translated into the common language of every nation unto which they come[18] that the Word of God dwelling plentifully in all, they may worship Him in an acceptable manner and through patience and comfort of the Scriptures may have hope.[19]

9. The infallible rule of interpretation of Scripture is the Scripture itself, and therefore, when there is a question about the true and full sense of any Scripture (which is not manifold, but one) it must be searched by other places that speak more clearly.[20]

10. The supreme Judge by Which all controversies of religion are to be determined, and all decrees of councils, opinions of ancient writers, doctrines of men, and private spirits are to be examined, and in whose sentence we are to rest can be no other but the Holy Scripture delivered by the Spirit, into which Scripture so delivered, our faith is finally resolved.[21]

---

16   Acts 15:15
17   John 5:39
18   1 Corinthians 14:6, 9, 11; 12:24, 28
19   Colossians 3:16
20   2 Peter 1:20-21; Acts 15:15-16
21   Matthew 22:29, 31; Ephesians 2:20; Acts 28:23

CHAPTER 2

THE HOLY TRINITY

1. The Lord our God is but one only living and true God,[1] Whose subsistence is in and of Himself;[2] infinite in being and perfection,[3] Whose essence cannot be comprehended by any but Himself; a most pure Spirit;[4] invisible;[5] without body, parts, or passions; Who only hath immortality; dwelling in the light which no man can approach unto; Who is immutable,[6] immense,[7] eternal, incomprehensible,[8] almighty, every way infinite,[9] most holy, most wise, most free, and most absolute,[10] working all things according to the council of His own immutable and most righteous will[11] for His own glory;[12] most loving, gracious, merciful, long-suffering, abundant in

---

1   1 Corinthians 8:4, 6; Deuteronomy 6:4
2   Jeremiah 10:10; Isaiah 48:12
3   Exodus 3:14
4   John 4:24
5   1 Timothy 1:17; Deuteronomy 4:15-16
6   Malachi 3:6
7   1 Kings 8:27; Jeremiah 23:23
8   Psalm 90:2
9   Genesis 17:1
10   Isaiah 6:3
11   Psalm 115:3; Isaiah 46:10
12   Proverbs 16:4; Romans 11:36

goodness and truth; forgiving iniquity, transgression, and sin; the Rewarder of them who diligently seek Him;[13] and withal, most just and terrible in His judgments;[14] hating all sin;[15] and Who will by no means clear the guilty.[16]

2. God, having all life,[17] glory,[18] goodness,[19] and blessedness in and of Himself is alone in and unto Himself all-sufficient, not standing in need of any creature which He hath made nor deriving any glory from them but only manifesting His own glory in, by, unto, and upon them;[20] He is alone the Fountain of all being, of Whom, through Whom, and to Whom are all things;[21] and He hath most sovereign dominion over all creatures to do by them, for them, or upon them whatsoever He pleases;[22] in His sight, all things are open and manifest;[23] His knowledge is infinite, infallible, and independent of the creature, so as nothing is to Him contingent or uncertain;[24] He is most holy in all His counsels, in all His works, and in all His commands;[25] to Him is due from angels and men

---

13   Exodus 34:6-7; Hebrews 11:6
14   Nehemiah 9:32-33
15   Psalm 5:5-6
16   Exodus 34:7; Nahum 1:2-3
17   John 5:26
18   Psalm 148:13
19   Psalm 119:68
20   Job 22:2,3
21   Romans 11:34-36
22   Daniel 4:25, 34-35
23   Hebrews 4:13
24   Ezekiel 11:5; Acts 15:18
25   Psalm 145:17

whatsoever worship, service, or obedience as creatures they owe unto the Creator and whatever He is further pleased to require of them.[26]

3. In this Divine and infinite Being, there are three subsistences: the Father, the Word (or Son), and the Holy Spirit, of one substance, power, and eternity, each having the whole Divine essence,[27] yet the essence undivided;[28] the Father is of none, neither begotten nor proceeding; the Son is eternally begotten of the Father;[29] the Holy Spirit proceeds from the Father and the Son;[30] all infinite, without beginning, therefore, but one God, Who is not to be divided in nature and being, but distinguished by several peculiar, relative properties and personal relations, which doctrine of the Trinity is the foundation of all our communion with God, and comfortable dependance on Him.

---

26 Revelation 5:12-14
27 Matthew 28:19; 2 Corinthians 13:14
28 Exodus 3:14; John 14:11; 1 Corinthians 8:6
29 John 1:14, 18
30 John 15:26; Galatians 4:6

CHAPTER 3

GOD'S DECREE

1. God hath decreed in Himself from all eternity by the most wise and holy counsel of His own will, freely and unchangeably, all things whatsoever comes to pass;[1] yet so as thereby is God neither the Author of sin, nor hath fellowship with any therein,[2] nor is violence offered to the will of the creature, nor yet is the liberty or contingency of second causes taken away but rather established,[3] in which appears His wisdom in disposing all things, and power, and faithfulness in accomplishing His decree.[4]

2. Although God knows whatsoever may or can come to pass upon all supposed conditions,[5] yet hath He not decreed anything because He foresaw it as future or as that which would come to pass upon such conditions.[6]

3. By the decree of God for the manifestation of His glory some men and angels are predestinated, or foreordained,

---

1 Isaiah 46:10; Ephesians 1:11; Hebrews 6:17; Romans 9:15, 18
2 James 1:15, 17; 1 John 1:5
3 Acts 4:27-28; John 19:11
4 Numbers 23:19; Ephesians 1:3-5
5 Acts 15:18
6 Romans 9:11, 13, 16, 18

to eternal life through Jesus Christ[7] to the praise of His glorious grace,[8] others being left to act in their sin to their just condemnation to the praise of His glorious justice.[9]

4. These angels and men thus predestinated and foreordained are particularly and unchangeably designed and their number so certain and definite that it cannot be either increased or diminished.[10]

5. Those of mankind who are predestinated to life,[11] God, before the foundation of the world was laid, according to His eternal and immutable purpose and the secret counsel and good pleasure of His will, hath chosen in Christ unto everlasting glory out of His mere free grace and love without any other thing in the creature as a condition or cause moving Him thereunto.[12]

6. As God hath appointed the elect unto glory, so He hath by the eternal and most free purpose of His will foreordained all the means thereunto;[13] wherefore, they who are elected, being fallen in Adam, are redeemed by Christ,[14] are effectually called unto faith in Christ by His Spirit working in due season,[15] are justified, adopted, sanctified, and kept by His

---

7   1 Timothy 5:21; Matthew 25:41
8   Ephesians 1:5-6
9   Romans 9:22-23; Judges 4
10 2 Timothy 2:19; John 13:18
11 Ephesians 1:4, 9, 11; Romans 8:30; 2 Timothy 1:9; 1 Thessalonians 5:9
12 Romans 9:13, 16; Ephesians 1:6, 12
13 1 Peter 1:2; 2 Thessalonians 2:13
14 1 Thessalonians 5:9-10
15 Romans 8:30; 2 Thessalonians 2:13

power through faith unto salvation;[16] neither are any other redeemed by Christ or effectually called, justified, adopted, sanctified, and saved, but the elect only.[17]

7. The doctrine of this high mystery of predestination is to be handled with special prudence and care, that men attending the will of God revealed in His Word and yielding obedience thereunto may from the certainty of their effectual vocation be assured of their eternal election;[18] so shall this doctrine afford matters of praise, reverence, and admiration of God[19] and of humility, diligence,[20] and abundant consolation to all that sincerely obey the Gospel.[21]

---

16 1 Peter 1:5
17 John 6:64; 10:26; 17:9
18 1 Thessalonians 1:4-5; 2 Peter 1:10
19 Ephesians 1:6; Romans 11:33
20 Romans 11:5-6
21 Luke 10:20

CHAPTER 4

CREATION

1. In the beginning, it pleased God the Father, Son, and Holy Spirit[1] for the manifestation of the glory of His eternal power, wisdom, and goodness[2] to create or make the world and all things therein, whether visible or invisible, in the space of six days, and all very good.[3]

2. After God had made all other creatures, He created man, male and female,[4] with reasonable and immortal souls,[5] rendering them fit unto that life to God for which they were created; being made after the image of God in knowledge, righteousness, and true holiness;[6] having the law of God written in their hearts and power to fulfill it;[7] and yet under a possibility of transgressing, being left to the liberty of their own will, which was subject to change.[8]

---

1   John 1:2-3; Hebrews 1:2; Job 26:13
2   Romans 1:20
3   Colossians 1:16; Genesis 2:1-2
4   Genesis 1:27
5   Genesis 2:7
6   Ecclesiastes 7:29; Genesis 1:26
7   Romans 2:14-15
8   Genesis 3:6

3. Besides the law written in their hearts, they received a command not to eat of the tree of knowledge of good and evil,[9] which whilst they kept, they were happy in their communion with God and had dominion over the creatures.[10]

---

9   Genesis 3:8-10; 6:17
10 Genesis 1:26, 28

CHAPTER 5

DIVINE PROVIDENCE

1. God, the good Creator of all things, in His infinite power and wisdom, doth uphold, direct, dispose, and govern all creatures and things,[1] from the greatest even to the least, by His most wise and holy Providence, to the end for the which they were created,[2] according unto His infallible foreknowledge and the free and immutable counsel of His own will, to the praise of the glory of His wisdom, power, justice, infinite goodness, and mercy.[3]

2. Although in relation to the foreknowledge and decree of God as the first cause, all things come to pass immutably and infallibly[4] so that nothing befalls any by chance or without His Providence;[5] yet by the same Providence, He orders them to fall out, according to the nature of second causes, either necessarily, freely, or contingently.[6]

---

1 Hebrews 1:3; Job 38:11; Isaiah 46:10-11; Psalm 135:6
2 Matthew 10:29-31
3 Ephesians 1:11
4 Acts 2:23
5 Proverbs 16:33
6 Genesis 8:22

3. God, in His ordinary Providence makes use of means[7] yet is free to work without,[8] above,[9] and against them at His pleasure.[10]

4. The almighty power, unsearchable wisdom, and infinite goodness of God so far manifest themselves in His Providence that His determinate counsel extends itself even to the first fall and all other sinful actions, both of angels and men (and that not by a bare permission),[11] which also He most wisely and powerfully bounds and otherwise orders and governs[12] in a manifold dispensation to His most holy ends;[13] yet so, as the sinfulness of their acts proceeds only from the creatures, and not from God, Who being most holy and righteous, neither is nor can be the Author or Approver of sin.[14]

5. The most wise, righteous, and gracious God doth oftentimes leave for a season His own children to manifold temptations and the corruptions of their own heart to chastise them for their former sins or to discover unto them the hidden strength of corruption and deceitfulness of their hearts that they may be humbled[15] and to raise them to a closer and more constant dependence for their support upon Himself and to make them more watchful against all future occasions of sin

---

7   Acts 27:31, 44; Isaiah 55:10-11
8   Hosea 1:7
9   Romans 4:19-21
10 Daniel 3:27
11 Romans 11:32-34; 2 Samuel 24:1; 1 Chronicles 21:1
12 2 Kings 19:28; Psalm 76:10
13 Genesis 50:20; Isaiah 10:6-7, 12
14 Psalm 50:21; 1 John 2:16
15 2 Chronicles 32:25-26, 31; 2 Samuel 24:1; 2 Corinthians 12:7-9

and for other just and holy ends, so that whatsoever befalls any of His elect is by His appointment, for His glory, and for their good.[16]

6. As for those wicked and ungodly men whom God as a righteous Judge for former sin doth blind and harden,[17] from them He not only withholds His grace, whereby they might have been enlightened in their understanding and wrought upon in their hearts,[18] but sometimes, also withdraws the gifts which they had[19] and exposes them to such objects as their corruptions make occasion of sin[20] and withal gives them over to their own lusts, the temptations of the world, and the power of Satan,[21] whereby it comes to pass that they harden themselves, even under those means which God uses for the softening of others.[22]

7. As the Providence of God doth in general reach to all creatures, so after a most special manner it taketh care of His Church and disposes of all things to the good thereof.[23]

16   Romans 8:28
17   Romans 1:24, 26, 28; 11:7-8
18   Deuteronomy 29:4
19   Matthew 13:12
20   Deuteronomy 2:30; 2 Kings 8:12-13
21   Psalm 81:11-12; 2 Thessalonians 2:10-12
22   Exodus 8:15, 32; Isaiah 6:9-10; 1 Peter 2:7-8
23   1 Timothy 4:10; Amos 9:8-9; Isaiah 43:3-5

CHAPTER 6

THE FALL OF MAN, SIN, AND THE PUNISHMENT THEREOF

1. Although God created man upright and perfect and gave him a righteous law which had been unto life had he kept it and threatened death upon the breach thereof,[1] he did not long abide in this honor; Satan used the subtilty of the serpent to seduce Eve, then by her seducing Adam, who without any compulsion did willfully transgress the law of their creation and the command given unto them in eating the forbidden fruit, which God was pleased according to His wise and holy counsel to permit, having purposed to order it to His own glory.[2]

2. Our first parents, by this sin, fell from their original righteousness and communion with God[3] and we in them, whereby death came upon all, all becoming dead in sin and wholly defiled[4] in all the faculties and parts of soul and body.[5]

---

1   Genesis 2:16-17
2   Genesis 3:12-13; 2 Corinthians 11:3
3   Romans 3:23
4   Romans 5:12
5   Titus 1:15; Genesis 6:5; Jeremiah 17:9; Romans 3:10-19

3. They being the root and by God's appointment standing in the room and stead of all mankind, the guilt of the sin was imputed and corrupted nature conveyed to all their posterity descending from them by ordinary generation,[6] being now conceived in sin[7] and by nature children of wrath,[8] the servants of sin, the subjects of death and all other miseries, spiritual, temporal, and eternal,[9] unless the Lord Jesus sets them free.[10]

4. From this original corruption, whereby we are utterly indisposed, disabled, and made opposite to all good and wholly inclined to all evil,[11] do proceed all actual transgressions.[12]

5. The corruption of nature during this life doth remain in those who are regenerated;[13] and although it be through Christ pardoned and mortified, yet both itself and the first motions thereof are truly and properly sin.[14]

---

6   Romans 5:12-19; 1 Corinthians 15:21-22, 45, 49
7   Psalm 51:5; Job 14:4
8   Ephesians 2:3
9   Romans 6:20, 5:12
10   Hebrews 2:14; 1 Thessalonians 1:10
11   Romans 8:7; Colossians 1:21
12   James 1:14-15; Matthew 15:19
13   Romans 7:18, 23; Ecclesiastes 7:20; 1 John 1:8
14   Romans 7:24-25; Galatians 5:17

CHAPTER 7

GOD'S COVENANT

1. The distance between God and the creature is so great that although reasonable creatures do owe obedience unto Him as their Creator, they could never have attained the reward of life but by some voluntary condescension on God's part.[1]

2. Moreover, man having brought himself under the curse of the law by his fall,[2] it pleased the Lord to offer to mankind life and salvation by Jesus Christ, requiring of them faith in Him that they may be saved[3] and promising to give unto all those who are ordained unto eternal life His Holy Spirit to make them willing and able to believe.[4]

3. This grace toward sinners is revealed in the Gospel, first of all to Adam in the promise of salvation by the seed of the woman[5] and afterward by further steps until the full discovery thereof was completed in the New Testament;[6]

---

1   Luke 17:10; Job 35:7-8
2   Genesis 2:17; Galatians 3:10; Romans 3:20-21
3   Romans 8:3; Mark 16:15-16; John 3:16
4   Ezekiel 36:26-27; John 6:44-45; Psalm 110:3
5   Genesis 3:15
6   Hebrews 1:1

and it is founded in that eternal pact between the Father and the Son about the redemption of the elect;[7] and it is alone by this grace that all of the posterity of fallen Adam that ever were saved did obtain life and a blessed immortality, man being now utterly incapable of acceptance with God upon those terms on which Adam stood in his state of innocency.[8]

---

7   2 Timothy 1:9; Titus 1:2
8   Hebrews 11:6, 13; Romans 4:1-2; Acts 4:12; John 8:56

CHAPTER 8

CHRIST THE MEDIATOR

1. It pleased God in His eternal purpose to choose and ordain the Lord Jesus, His only begotten Son, in accordance with Their eternal pact, to be the Mediator between God and man;[1] the Prophet,[2] Priest,[3] and King;[4] Head and Savior of His Church; the Heir of all things; and Judge of the world, unto whom He did from all eternity give a people to be His seed and to be by Him in time redeemed, called, justified, sanctified, and glorified.[5]

2. The Son of God, the second Person in the Holy Trinity, being very and eternal God, the brightness of the Father's glory, of one substance and equal with Him, Who made the world, Who upholds and governs all things He hath made, did, when the fullness of time was come, take unto Him man's nature with all the essential properties and common

---

1 Isaiah 42:1; 1 Peter 1:19-20
2 Acts 3:22
3 Hebrews 5:5-6
4 Psalm 2:6; Luke 1:33; Ephesians 1:23; Hebrews 1:2; Acts 17:31
5 Isaiah 53:10; John 17:6; Romans 8:30

infirmities thereof,[6] yet without sin,[7] being conceived by the Holy Spirit in the womb of the virgin Mary, the Holy Spirit coming down upon her and the power of the Most High overshadowing her, and so was made of a woman, of the tribe of Judah, of the seed of Abraham and David according to the Scriptures;[8] so that two whole, perfect, and distinct natures were inseparably joined together in one Person without conversion, composition, or confusion, which person is very God and very man, yet one Christ, the only Mediator between God and man.[9]

3. The Lord Jesus in His human nature thus united to the Divine in the Person of the Son, was sanctified and anointed with the Holy Spirit above measure,[10] having in Him all the treasures of wisdom and knowledge,[11] in Whom it pleased the Father that all fullness should dwell[12] to the end that being holy, harmless, undefiled,[13] and full of grace and truth,[14] He might be thoroughly furnished to execute the office of a Mediator and Surety,[15] which office He took not upon Himself, but was thereunto called by His Father,[16] Who

6   John 1:1,14; Galatians 4:4
7   Romans 8:3; Hebrews 2:14, 16-17; 4:15
8   Luke 1:27, 31, 35
9   Romans 9:5; 1 Timothy 2:5
10   Psalm 45:7; Acts 10:38; John 3:34
11   Colossians 2:3
12   Colossians 1:19
13   Hebrews 7:26
14   John 1:14
15   Hebrews 7:22
16   Hebrews 5:5

also put all power and judgment in His hand and gave Him commandment to execute the same.[17]

4. This office the Lord Jesus did most willingly undertake,[18] that He might discharge He was made under the Law and did perfectly fulfill it[19] and underwent the punishment due to us, which we should have borne and suffered,[20] being made sin and a curse for us;[21] enduring most grievous sorrows in His soul and most painful sufferings in His body;[22] was crucified, and died, and remained in the state of the dead; yet saw no corruption;[23] on the third day, He arose from the dead[24] with the same body in which He suffered;[25] with which He also ascended into Heaven,[26] and there sits at the right hand of His Father making intercession;[27] and shall return to judge men and angels at the end of the age.[28]

5. The Lord Jesus, by His perfect obedience and sacrifice of Himself, which He through the eternal Spirit once offered up unto God, hath fully satisfied the justice of God,[29] procured

---

17   John 5:22, 27; Matthew 28:18; Acts 2:36
18   Psalm 40:7-8; Hebrews 10:5-11; John 10:18
19   Galatians 4:4; Matthew 3:15
20   Galatians 3:13; Isaiah 53:6; 1 Peter 3:18
21   2 Corinthians 5:21
22   Matthew 26:37-38; Luke 22:44; Matthew 27:46
23   Acts 13:37
24   1 Corinthians 15:3-4
25   John 20:25, 27
26   Mark 16:19; Acts 1:9-11
27   Romans 8:34; Hebrews 9:24
28   Acts 10:42; Romans 14:9-10; Acts 1:10
29   Hebrews 9:14; 10:14; Romans 3:25-26

reconciliation, and purchased an everlasting inheritance in the Kingdom of Heaven for all those whom the Father hath given unto Him.[30]

6. Although the price of redemption was not actually paid by Christ till after His incarnation; yet the virtue, efficacy, and benefit thereof were communicated to the elect in all ages successively from the beginning of the world;[31] in and by those promises, types, and sacrifices wherein He was revealed; and signified to be the Seed of the woman which should bruise the serpent's head; and the Lamb slain from the foundation of the world;[32] being the same yesterday, and today, and forever.[33]

7. Christ, in the work of mediation, acteth according to both natures, by each nature doing that which is proper to itself; yet by reason of the unity of the Person, that which is proper to one nature is sometimes in Scripture attributed to the Person denominated by the other nature.[34]

8. To all those for whom Christ hath obtained eternal redemption, He doth certainly and effectually apply and communicate the same;[35] making intercession for them; uniting them to Himself by His Spirit; revealing unto them, in

---

30   John 17:2; Hebrews 9:15
31   1 Corinthians 4:10; Hebrews 4:2; 1 Peter 1:10-11
32   Revelation 13:8
33   Hebrews 13:8
34   John 3:13; Acts 20:28
35   John 6:37; 10:15-16; 17:9; Romans 5:10

and by the Word, the mystery of salvation;[36] persuading them to believe and obey; governing their hearts by His Word and Spirit;[37] and overcoming all their enemies by His almighty power and wisdom[38] in such manner and ways as are most consonant to His wonderful and unsearchable dispensation and all of free and absolute grace, without any condition foreseen in them to procure it.[39]

9. This office of Mediator between God and man is proper only to Christ, Who is the Prophet, Priest, and King of the Church of God, and may not be either in whole or any part thereof transferred from Him to any other.[40]

10. This number and order of offices is necessary; for in respect of our ignorance, we stand in need of His prophetical office;[41] and in respect of our alienation from God and imperfection of the best of our services, we need His priestly office to reconcile us and present us acceptable unto God;[42] and in respect of our averseness and utter inability to return to God, and for our rescue and security from our spiritual adversaries, we need His kingly office to convince, subdue, draw, uphold, deliver, and preserve us to His Heavenly Kingdom.[43]

---

36 John 17:6; Ephesians 1:9; 1 John 5:20
37 Romans 8:9, 14
38 Psalm 110:1; 1 Corinthians 15:25-26
39 John 3:8; Ephesians 1:8
40 1 Timothy 2:5
41 John 1:18
42 Colossians 1:21; Galatians 5:17
43 John 16:8; Psalm 110:3; Luke 1:74-75

CHAPTER 9

FREE WILL

1. God hath endued the will of man with that natural liberty and power of acting upon choice; that it is neither forced nor by any necessity of nature determined to do good or evil.[1]

2. Man, in his state of innocence, had freedom and power to will and to do that which was good and well-pleasing to God[2] but yet was mutable, so that he might fall from it.[3]

3. Man, by his fall into a state of sin, hath wholly lost all ability of will to any spiritual good accompanying salvation,[4] so as a natural man, being altogether averse from that good and dead in sin,[5] is not able, by his own strength, to convert himself or to prepare himself thereunto.[6]

4. When God converts a sinner and translates him into the state of grace, He frees him from his natural bondage under

---

1   Matthew 17:12; James 1:14; Deuteronomy 30:19
2   Ecclesiastes 7:29
3   Genesis 3:6
4   Romans 5:6; 8:7
5   Ephesians 2:1-5
6   Titus 3:3-5; John 6:44

sin,[7] and by His grace alone, enables him freely to will and to do that which is spiritually good;[8] yet so as that by reason of his remaining corruptions, he doth not perfectly nor only will that which is good but doth also will that which is evil.[9]

5. The will of man is made perfectly and immutably free to good alone, in the state of glory only.[10]

---

7   Colossians 1:13; John 8:36
8   Philippians 2:13
9   Romans 7:15, 18-19, 21, 23
10   Ephesians 4:13

CHAPTER 10

EFFECTUAL CALLING

1. Those whom God hath predestinated unto life, He is pleased, in His appointed and accepted time, effectually to call by His Word and Spirit out of that state of sin and death, in which they are by nature,[1] to grace and salvation by Jesus Christ;[2] enlightening their minds spiritually and savingly to understand the things of God;[3] taking away their heart of stone and giving unto them a heart of flesh;[4] renewing their wills and by His almighty power determining them to that which is good[5] and effectually drawing them to Jesus Christ; yet so as they come most freely, being made willing by His grace.[6]

2. This effectual call is of God's free and special grace alone, not from anything at all foreseen in man[7] nor from any power or agency in the creature coworking with His special

---

1   Romans 8:30; 11:7; Ephesians 1:10-11; 2 Thessalonians 3:13-14
2   Ephesians 2:1-6
3   Acts 26:18; Ephesians 1:17-18
4   Ezekiel 36:26
5   Deuteronomy 30:6; Ezekiel 36:27; Ephesians 1:19
6   Psalm 110:3
7   2 Timothy 1:9; Ephesians 2:8

grace; the creature being wholly passive therein, being dead in sins and trespasses until being quickened and renewed by the Holy Spirit, he is thereby enabled to answer this call and to embrace the grace offered and conveyed in it [8] and that by no less power than that which raised up Christ from the dead.[9]

3. Elect infants dying in infancy are regenerated and saved by Christ through the Spirit,[10] Who worketh when and where and how He pleases;[11] so also are all other persons who are incapable of being outwardly called by the ministry of the Word.

4. Others not elected, although they may be called by the ministry of the Word and may have some common operations of the Spirit,[12] yet not being effectually drawn by the Father, neither will nor can truly come to Christ,[13] and therefore, cannot be saved; much less can men who receive not the Christian religion be saved, be they ever so diligent to frame their lives according to the light of nature and the law of that religion they do profess.[14]

---

8   1 Corinthians 2:14; Ephesians 2:5; John 5:25
9   Ephesians 1:19-20
10 John 3:3, 5-6
11 John 3:8
12 Matthew 13:20-21; 22:14; Hebrews 6:4-5
13 John 6:44-45, 65; 1 John 2:24-25
14 Acts 4:12; John 4:22; 17:3

CHAPTER 11

JUSTIFICATION

1. Those whom God effectually calls He also freely justifies,[1] not by infusing righteousness into them but by pardoning their sins[2] and by accounting and accepting their persons as righteous;[3] not for anything wrought in them, or done by them, but for Christ's sake alone; not by imputing faith itself, the act of believing, or any other evangelical obedience to them as their righteousness; but by imputing Christ's active obedience unto the whole law and passive obedience in His death for their whole and sole righteousness,[4] they, receiving and resting on Him and His righteousness by faith, which faith they have not of themselves, it is the gift of God.[5]

2. Faith, thus receiving and resting on Christ and His righteousness, is the alone instrument of justification;[6] yet it is not alone in the person justified but is ever accompanied

1 Romans 3:24; 8:30
2 Romans 4:5-8; Ephesians 1:7
3 1 Corinthians 1:30-31; Romans 5:17-19
4 Philippians 3:8-9
5 John 1:12; Romans 5:17; Ephesians 2:8-10
6 Romans 3:28

with all other saving graces and is no dead faith but worketh by love.[7]

3. Christ, by His obedience and death, did fully discharge the debt of all those who are justified and did, by the sacrifice of Himself in the blood of His cross, undergoing in their stead the penalty due unto them, make a proper, real, and full satisfaction to God's justice on their behalf;[8] yet inasmuch as He was given by the Father for them, and His obedience and satisfaction accepted in their stead, and both freely, not for anything in them; their justification is only of free grace,[9] that both the exact justice and rich grace of God might be glorified in the justification of sinners.[10]

4. God did, from all eternity, decree to justify all the elect,[11] and Christ did, in the fullness of time, die for their sins and rise again for their justification;[12] nevertheless, they are not justified personally until the Holy Spirit doth in due time actually apply Christ unto them.[13]

5. God doth continue to forgive the sins of those who are justified,[14] and although they can never fall from the state of justification,[15] yet they may, by their sins, fall under God's

7   Galatians 5:6; James 2:17, 22, 26
8   Hebrews 10:14; 1 Peter 1:18-19; Isaiah 53:5-6
9   Romans 8:32; 2 Corinthians 5:21
10   Romans 3:26; Ephesians 1:6-7; 2:7
11   Galatians 3:8; 1 Peter 1:2; 1 Timothy 2:6
12   Romans 4:25
13   Colossians 1:21-22; Titus 3:4-7
14   Matthew 6:12; 1 John 1:7, 9
15   John 10:28

Fatherly displeasure;[16] and in that condition, they have not usually the light of His countenance restored unto them until they humble themselves, confess their sins, beg pardon, renew their faith, and repent.[17]

6. The justification of believers under the Old Testament was in all these respects one and the same with the justification of believers under the New Testament.[18]

---

16   Psalm 89:31-33
17   Psalm 32:5, 51; Matthew 26:75
18   Galatians 3:9; Romans 4:22-24

CHAPTER 12

ADOPTION

1. All those who are justified, God vouchsafed, in and for the sake of His only Son Jesus Christ, to make partakers of the grace of adoption,[1] by which they are taken into the number, and enjoy the liberties and privileges of children of God;[2] have His name put upon them,[3] receive the spirit of adoption,[4] have access to the throne of grace with boldness, are enabled to cry, "Abba, Father,"[5] are pitied,[6] protected,[7] provided for,[8] and chastened by Him, as by a Father;[9] yet never cast off;[10] but sealed to the day of redemption[11] and inherit the promises as heirs of everlasting salvation.[12]

---

1   Ephesians 1:5; Galatians 4:4-5
2   John 1:12; Romans 8:17
3   2 Corinthians 6:18; Revelation 3:12
4   Romans 8:15
5   Galatians 4:6; Ephesians 2:18
6   Psalm 103:13
7   Proverbs 14:26
8   1 Peter 5:7
9   Hebrews 12:6
10   Isaiah 54:8-9; Lamentations 3:31
11   Ephesians 4:30
12   Hebrews 1:14; 6:12

CHAPTER 13

SANCTIFICATION

1. They who are united to Christ, effectually called and regenerated, having a new heart and a new spirit created in them through the virtue of Christ's death and resurrection, are also further sanctified really and personally through the same virtue[1] by His Word and Spirit dwelling in them;[2] the dominion of the whole body of sin is destroyed,[3] and the several lusts thereof are more and more weakened and mortified;[4] and they are more and more quickened and strengthened in all saving graces[5] to the practice of all true holiness, without which no man shall see the Lord.[6]

2. This sanctification is throughout, in the whole man,[7] yet imperfect in this life;[8] there abides still some remnants of corruption in every part, whence arises a continual and

---

1   Acts 20:32; Romans 6:5-6
2   John 17:17; Ephesians 3:16-19; 1 Thessalonians 5:21-23
3   Romans 6:14
4   Galatians 5:24
5   Colossians 1:11
6   2 Corinthians 7:1; Hebrews 12:14
7   1 Thessalonians 5:23
8   Romans 7:18, 23

irreconcilable war; the flesh lusting against the spirit, and the spirit against the flesh.[9]

3. In which war, although the remaining corruption, for a time may much prevail,[10] yet through the continual supply of strength from the sanctifying Spirit of Christ, the regenerate part doth overcome[11] and so the saints grow in grace, perfecting holiness in the fear of God, pressing after a heavenly life in evangelical obedience to all the commands, which Christ as Head and King in His Word hath prescribed to them.[12]

---

9   Galatians 5:17; 1 Peter 2:11
10 Romans 7:23
11 Romans 6:14
12 Ephesians 4:15-16; 2 Corinthians 3:18; 7:1

CHAPTER 14

SAVING FAITH

1. The grace of faith, whereby the elect are enabled to believe to the saving of their souls, is the work of the Spirit of Christ in their hearts[1] and is ordinarily wrought by the ministry of the word,[2] by which also and by the administration of baptism and the Lord's Supper, prayer, and other means appointed of God, it is increased and strengthened.[3]

2. By this faith, a Christian believeth to be true whatsoever is revealed in the Word for the authority of God Himself[4] and also apprehendeth an excellency therein above all other writings and all things in the world[5] as it bears forth the glory of God in His attributes, the excellency of Christ in His nature and offices, and the power and fullness of the Holy Spirit in His workings and operations and so is enabled to cast his soul upon the truth thus believed[6] and also acteth differently upon that which each particular passage thereof

---

1   2 Corinthians 4:13; Ephesians 2:8
2   Romans 10:14, 17
3   Luke 17:5; 1 Peter 2:2; Acts 20:32
4   Acts 24:14
5   Psalm 19:7-10, 119:72
6   2 Timothy 1:12

containeth, yielding obedience to the commands,[7] trembling at the threatenings,[8] and embracing the promises of God for this life and that which is to come;[9] but the principal acts of saving faith have immediate relation to Christ, accepting, receiving, and resting upon Him alone for justification, sanctification, and eternal life by virtue of His grace.[10]

3. This faith, although it be different in degrees and may be weak or strong,[11] yet it is in the least degree of it different in the kind or nature of it (as is all other saving grace) from the faith and common grace of temporary believers;[12] and therefore, though it may be many times assailed and weakened, yet it gets the victory;[13] growing up in many to the attainment of a full assurance through Christ,[14] Who is both the Author and Finisher of our faith.[15]

---

7   John 15:14
8   Isaiah 66:2
9   Hebrews 11:13
10 John 1:12; Acts 16:31; Galatians 2:20; Acts 15:11
11 Hebrews 5:13-14; Matthew 6:30; Romans 4:19-20
12 2 Peter 1:1
13 Ephesians 6:16; 1 John 5:4-5
14 Hebrews 6:11-12; Colossians 2:2
15 Hebrews 12:2

CHAPTER 15

REPENTANCE UNTO LIFE AND SALVATION

1. Such of the elect as are converted at riper years, having for some time lived in the state of nature and therein served divers lusts and pleasures, God in their effectual calling giveth them repentance unto life.[1]

2. Whereas there is none that doth good and sins not[2] and the best of men may through the power and deceitfulness of their corruption dwelling in them, with the prevalence of temptation, fall into great sins and provocations, God hath, in His grace, mercifully provided that believers so sinning and falling be renewed through repentance unto salvation.[3]

3. This saving repentance is an evangelical grace, whereby a person being by the Holy Spirit made sensible of the manifold evils of his sin, doth, by faith in Christ, humble himself for it with godly sorrow, detestation of it, and self-abhorrence;[4]

---

1   Titus 3:2-5
2   Ecclesiastes 7:20
3   Luke 22:31-32
4   Zechariah 12:10; Acts 11:18

praying for pardon and strength of grace[5] with a purpose and endeavor by supplies of the Spirit to walk before God unto all well-pleasing in all things.[6]

4. As repentance is to be continued through the whole course of our lives upon the account of the body of death and the motions thereof, so it is every man's duty to repent of his particular known sins.[7]

5. Such is the provision which God hath made through Christ in His grace for the preservation of believers unto salvation, that although there is no sin so small, but it deserves damnation,[8] yet there is no sin so great that it shall bring damnation on them who repent, which makes the constant preaching of repentance necessary.[9]

---

5   Ezekiel 36:31; 2 Corinthians 7:11
6   Psalm 119:6, 128
7   Luke 19:8; 1 Timothy 1:13, 15
8   Romans 6:23
9   Isaiah 1:16, 18; 55:7

CHAPTER 16

GOOD WORKS

1. Good works are only such as God hath commanded in His holy Word[1] and not such as without the warrant thereof are devised by men out of blind zeal or upon any pretense of good intentions.[2]

2. These good works, done in obedience to God's commandments, are the fruits and evidences of a true and lively faith;[3] and by them, believers manifest their thankfulness,[4] strengthen their assurance,[5] edify their brethren,[6] adorn the profession of the Gospel, stop the mouths of the adversaries, and glorify God,[7] Whose workmanship they are, created in Christ Jesus thereunto,[8] that having their fruit unto holiness, they may have the end eternal life.[9]

---

1   Micah 6:8; Hebrews 13:21
2   Matthew 15:9; Isaiah 29:13
3   James 2:18, 22
4   Psalm 116:12-13
5   1 John 2:3, 5; 2 Peter 1:5-11
6   Matthew 5:16
7   1 Timothy 6:1; 1 Peter 2:15; Philippians 1:11
8   Ephesians 2:10
9   Romans 6:22

3. Their ability to do good works is not at all of themselves, but wholly from the Spirit of Christ,[10] and that they may be enabled thereunto, besides the graces they have already received; there is necessary an actual influence of the same Holy Spirit to work in them to will and to do of His good pleasure;[11] yet are they not hereupon to grow negligent, as if they were not bound to perform any duty unless upon a special motion of the Spirit; but they ought to be diligent in stirring up the grace of God that is in them.[12]

4. They who in their obedience attain to the greatest height which is possible in this life are so far from being able to supererogate and to do more than God requires, as that they fall short of much which in duty they are bound to do.[13]

5. We cannot by our best works merit pardon of sin or eternal life at the hand of God by reason of the great disproportion that is between them and the glory to come and the infinite distance that is between us and God, and by these works, we can neither profit nor satisfy for the debt of our former sins;[14] but when we have done all we can, we have done but our duty and are unprofitable servants; and because as they are good, they proceed from His Spirit;[15] and as they

10   John 15:4, 6
11   2 Corinthians 3:5; Philippians 2:13
12   Philippians 2:12; Hebrews 6:11-12; Isaiah 64:7
13   Job 9:2-3; Galatians 5:17; Luke 17:10
14   Romans 3:20; Ephesians 2:8-9; Romans 4:6
15   Galatians 5:22,23

are wrought by us, they are defiled and mixed with so much weakness and imperfection that they cannot endure the severity of God's judgment.[16]

6. Yet notwithstanding, the persons of believers being accepted through Christ, their good works also are accepted in Him,[17] not as though they were in this life wholly unblameable and unreprovable in God's sight but that He looking upon them in His Son is pleased to accept and reward that which is sincere, although accompanied with many weaknesses and imperfections.[18]

7. Works done by unregenerate men, although for the matter of them they may be things which God commands and of good use both to themselves and others;[19] yet because they proceed not from a heart purified by faith,[20] nor are done in a right manner according to the Word,[21] nor to a right end the glory of God;[22] they are therefore sinful and cannot please God; nor make a man meet to receive grace from God;[23] and yet their neglect of them is more sinful and displeasing to God.[24]

---

16   Isaiah 64:6; Psalm 143:2
17   Ephesians 1:6; 1 Peter 2:5
18   Matthew 25:21, 23; Hebrews 6:10
19   2 Kings 10:30; 1 Kings 21:27, 29
20   Genesis 4:5; Hebrews 11:4, 6
21   1 Corinthians 13:1
22   Matthew 6:2, 5
23   Amos 5:21-22; Romans 9:16; Titus 3:5
24   Job 21:14, 15; Matthew 25:41-43

CHAPTER 17

PERSEVERANCE
OF THE SAINTS

1. Those whom God hath accepted in the beloved, effectually called and sanctified by His Spirit and given the precious faith of His elect unto, can neither totally nor finally fall from the state of grace but shall certainly persevere therein to the end and be eternally saved, seeing the gifts and callings of God are without repentance (whence He still begets and nourishes in them faith, repentance, love, joy, hope, and all the graces of the Spirit unto immortality);[1] and though many storms and floods arise and beat against them, yet they shall never be able to take them off that foundation and rock which by faith they are fastened upon: notwithstanding through unbelief and the temptations of Satan the sensible sight of the light and love of God may, for a time, be clouded and obscured from them;[2] yet He is still the same, and they shall be sure to be kept by the power of God unto salvation, where they shall enjoy their purchased possession, they being engraven upon

1   John 10:28-29; Philippians 1:6; 2 Timothy 2:19; 1 John 2:19
2   Psalm 89:31-32; 1 Corinthians 11:32

the palm of His hands and their names having been written in the Book of Life from all eternity.[3]

2. This perseverance of the saints depends not upon their own free will but upon the immutability of the decree of election flowing from the free and unchangeable love of God the Father,[4] upon the efficacy of the merit and intercession of Jesus Christ and union with Him,[5] the oath of God,[6] the abiding of His Spirit and the seed of God within them,[7] and the nature of the grace from which arises also the certainty and infallibility thereof.[8]

3. And though they may, through the temptation of Satan and of the world, the prevalence of corruption remaining in them and the neglect of means of their preservation fall into grievous sins and for a time continue therein;[9] whereby they incur God's displeasure and grieve His Holy Spirit,[10] come to have their graces and comforts impaired,[11] have their hearts hardened and their consciences wounded, [12] hurt and scandalize others, and bring temporal judgments upon

---

3   Malachi 3:6
4   Romans 8:30; 9:11, 16
5   Romans 5:9-10; John 14:19
6   Hebrews 6:17-18
7   1 John 3:9
8   Jeremiah 32:40
9   Matthew 26:70, 72, 74
10 Isaiah 64:5, 9; Ephesians 4:30
11 Psalm 51:10, 12
12 Psalm 32:3-4

themselves;[13] yet they shall ultimately be preserved through faith in Christ Jesus to the end.[14]

13   2 Samuel 12:14
14   Luke 22:32, 61-62

CHAPTER 18

ASSURANCE OF GRACE AND SALVATION

1. Although temporary believers and other unregenerate men may vainly deceive themselves with false hopes and carnal presumptions of being in the favor of God and state of salvation, which hope of theirs shall perish;[1] yet such as truly believe in the Lord Jesus and love Him in sincerity, endeavoring to walk in all good conscience before Him, may in this life be certainly assured that they are in the state of grace[2] and may rejoice in the hope of the glory of God, Which hope shall never make them ashamed.[3]

2. This certainty is not a bare conjectural and probable persuasion grounded upon a fallible hope[4] but an infallible assurance of faith founded on the blood and righteousness of Christ revealed in the Gospel[5] and also upon the inward evidence of those graces of the Spirit unto which promises

---

1   Job 8:13-14; Matthew 7:22-23
2   1 John 2:3; 3:14, 18-19, 21, 24; 5:13
3   Romans 5:2, 5
4   Hebrews 6:11, 19
5   Hebrews 6:17-18

are made,[6] and on the testimony of the Spirit of adoption witnessing with our Spirits that we are the children of God,[7] and as a fruit thereof keeping the heart both humble and holy.[8]

3. This infallible assurance doth not so belong to the essence of faith but that a true believer may wait long and conflict with many difficulties before he be a partaker of it;[9] yet being enabled by the Spirit to know the things which are freely given him of God,[10] he may without extraordinary revelation in the right use of means attain thereunto;[11] and therefore, it is the duty of every one to give all diligence to make their calling and election sure, that thereby his heart may be enlarged in peace and joy in the Holy Spirit, in love and thankfulness to God and in strength and cheerfulness in the duties of obedience, the proper fruits of this assurance,[12] so far is it from inclining men to looseness.[13]

4. True believers may have the assurance of their salvation by divers ways shaken, diminished, and intermitted; as by negligence in preserving of it, by falling into some special sin which wounds the conscience and grieves the Spirit,[14] by some

---

6   2 Peter 1:4-5, 10-11
7   Romans 8:15-16
8   1 John 3:1-3
9   Isaiah 50:10; Psalm 77:1-12; 88
10 1 John 4:13; Hebrews 6:11-12
11 Romans 5:1, 2, 5, 14, 17; Psalm 119:32
12 Romans 5:1, 2, 5; 14:17; Psalm 119:32
13 Romans 6:1,2; Titus 2:11,12,14
14 Psalm 51:8, 12, 14

sudden or vehement temptation,[15] by God's withdrawing the light of His countenance and suffering even such as fear Him to walk in darkness and to have no light;[16] yet are they never destitute of the seed of God[17] and life of faith,[18] that love of Christ and the brethren, and that sincerity of heart and conscience of duty, out of which by the operation of the Spirit this assurance may in due time be revived;[19] and by the which, in the meantime, they are preserved from utter despair.[20]

15   Psalm 116:11; 77:7-8; 31:22
16   Psalm 30:7
17   1 John 3:9
18   Luke 22:32
19   Psalm 42:5, 11
20   Lamentations 3:26-31

CHAPTER 19

THE LAW OF GOD

1. God gave to Adam a law of universal obedience written in his heart and a particular precept of not eating the fruit of the tree of knowledge of good and evil,[1] by which He bound him and all his posterity to personal, entire, exact, and perpetual obedience;[2] promised life upon the fulfilling; and threatened death upon the breach of it; and endued him with power and ability to keep it.[3]

2. God also gave a law to Israel, His elect nation under the Old Covenant, which was delivered to them from Mount Sinai in Ten Commandments and written in two tablets, the first four containing their duties toward God and the other six containing their duties toward man.[4]

3. Besides these Ten Commandments, this law also contained many statutes and ordinances, partly of worship prefiguring Christ and His graces, actions, sufferings, and

---

1   Genesis 1:27; Ecclesiastes 7:29
2   Romans 10:5
3   Galatians 3:10, 12
4   Deuteronomy 10:4

benefits,[5] and partly holding forth divers instructions of moral duties, and partly of judicial matters, but all being appointed only to the time of reformation were by the coming of Jesus Christ, the true Messiah and only Lawgiver, Who was furnished with power from the Father for that end, fulfilled and taken away.[6]

4. This does not leave God's people without a law, however, for in this age they are bound by the Law of Christ, the obligations of which are expounded in the New Testament Scriptures.[7]

5. Moreover, the law of the Old Covenant has a use in this age as a schoolmaster, in that it reveals the sinful pollutions of human nature, hearts, and lives, so as examining themselves thereby men may come to further conviction of, humiliation for, and hatred against sin, together with a clearer sight of the need they have of Christ and the perfection of His obedience;[8] it is likewise useful to the regenerate to restrain their corruptions, in that it forbids sin; and the threatenings of it serve to show what even their sins deserve and what afflictions in this life they may expect for them, although freed from the curse and unallayed rigor thereof. The promises of it

---

5   Hebrews 10:1; Colossians 2:17
6   Colossians 2:14, 16-17; Galatians 3:24-25; Ephesians 2:14, 16
7   John 13:34; 1 Corinthians 9:20-21
8   Romans 6:14; Galatians 2:16; Romans 8:1; 10:4

likewise show them God's approbation of obedience and what blessings they may expect upon the performance thereof.[9]

7. Neither are the forementioned uses of that law contrary to the grace of the Gospel, but do sweetly comply with it,[10] the spirit of Christ subduing and enabling the will of man through it and teaching him to do that freely and cheerfully what the will of God requires in this age.[11]

9   Romans 3:20; 7:7
10   Galatians 3:21
11   Ezekiel 36:27

CHAPTER 20

THE GOSPEL

1. Man's communion with God being broken by sin, God was pleased to give forth the promise of Christ, the Seed of the woman, as the means of calling the elect and begetting in them faith and repentance;[1] in this promise, the Gospel, as to the substance of it, was revealed and therein effectual for the conversion and salvation of sinners.[2]

2. This promise of Christ and salvation by Him is revealed only by the Word of God;[3] neither do the works of creation or Providence, with the light of nature, make discovery of Christ or of grace by Him so much as in a general or obscure way,[4] much less that men destitute of the revelation of Him by the promise or Gospel should be enabled thereby to attain saving faith or repentance.[5]

3. The revelation of the Gospel unto sinners, made in divers times and by sundry parts, with the addition of promises

---

1   Genesis 3:15
2   Revelation 13:8
3   Romans 1:17
4   Romans 10:14-15, 17
5   Proverbs 29:18; Isaiah 25:7; 60:2-3

and precepts for the obedience required therein, as to the nations and persons to whom it is granted, is merely of the Sovereign will and good pleasure of God;[6] not being annexed by virtue of any promise to the due improvement of man's natural abilities, by virtue of common light received without it, which none ever did make, or can do so.[7] And therefore, in all ages, the preaching of the Gospel hath been granted unto persons and nations, as to the extent or straightening of it, in great variety according to the counsel of the will of God.

4. Although the Gospel is the only outward means of revealing Christ and saving grace and is, as such, abundantly sufficient thereunto, yet that men who are dead in trespasses may be born again, quickened, or regenerated, there is moreover necessary an effectual, insuperable work of the Holy Spirit upon the whole soul for producing in them a new spiritual life,[8] without which no other means will affect their conversion unto God.[9]

---

6   Psalm 147:20; Acts 16:7
7   Romans 1:18
8   Psalm 110:3; 1 Corinthians 2:14; Ephesians 1:19-20
9   John 6:44; 2 Corinthians 4:4-6

CHAPTER 21

CHRISTIAN LIBERTY AND LIBERTY OF CONSCIENCE

1. The liberty which Christ hath purchased for believers under the Gospel consists in their freedom from the guilt of sin, the condemning wrath of God, the rigor and curse of the law;[1] and in their being delivered from this present evil world,[2] bondage to Satan,[3] and dominion of sin;[4] from the evil of afflictions,[5] the fear and sting of death,[6] the victory of the grave, and everlasting damnation;[7] as also in their free access to God;[8] and their yielding obedience unto Him not out of a slavish fear but a childlike love and willing mind,[9] all which were common also to believers under the Mosaic Law for the substance of them;[10] but under the New Testament, the liberty of Christians is further enlarged by their freedom

---

1   Galatians 3:13
2   Galatians 1:4
3   Acts 26:18
4   Romans 8:3
5   Romans 8:28
6   1 Corinthians 15:54-57
7   2 Thessalonians 1:10
8   Romans 8:15
9   Luke 1:74-75; 1 John 4:18
10 Galatians 3:9, 14

from the yoke of that law, and in greater boldness of access to the throne of grace, and in fuller communications of the Holy Spirit of God than believers under the law did partake of.[11]

2. God alone is Lord of the conscience[12] and hath left it free from the doctrines and commandments of men, which are in anything contrary to His Word or not contained in it.[13] So that to believe such doctrines or obey such commands against one's conscience is to betray true liberty of conscience;[14] and the requiring of an implicit faith and absolute and blind obedience is to destroy liberty of conscience and reason also.[15]

3. They who upon pretense of Christian liberty do practice any sin or cherish any sinful lust, as they do thereby pervert the main design of the grace of the Gospel to their own destruction,[16] so they wholly destroy the end of Christian liberty, which is, that being delivered out of the hands of all our enemies we might serve the Lord without fear in holiness and righteousness before Him all the days of our life.[17]

---

11 John 7:38-39; Hebrews 10:19-21
12 James 4:12; Romans 14:4
13 Acts 4:19; 5:29; 1 Corinthians 7:23; Matthew 15:9
14 Colossians 2:20, 22-23
15 1 Corinthians 3:5; 2 Corinthians 1:24
16 Romans 6:1-2
17 Galatians 5:13; 2 Peter 2:18-21

CHAPTER 22

RELIGIOUS WORSHIP

1. The light of nature shows that there is a God Who hath lordship and sovereignty over all; is just, good, and doth good unto all; and is therefore to be feared, loved, praised, called upon, trusted in, and served with all the heart and all the soul and with all the might.[1] But the acceptable way of worshipping the true God is instituted by Himself[2] and so limited by His own revealed will that He may not be worshipped according to the imaginations and devices of men, or the suggestions of Satan, or under any visible representations, or any other way not prescribed in the Holy Scriptures.[3]

2. Religious worship is to be given to God the Father, Son, and Holy Spirit, and to Him alone;[4] not to angels, saints, or any other creatures;[5] and since the fall not without a mediator[6] nor in the mediation of any other but Christ alone.[7]

---

1   Jeremiah 10:7; Mark 12:33
2   Deuteronomy 12:32
3   Exodus 20:4-6
4   Matthew 4:9-10; John 6:23; Matthew 28:19
5   Romans 1:25; Colossians 2:18; Revelation 19:10
6   John 14:6
7   1 Timothy 2:5

3. Prayer with thanksgiving, being one special part of natural worship, is by God required of all men.[8] But that it may be accepted, it is to be made in the name of the Son,[9] by the help of the Spirit,[10] according to His will with understanding, reverence, humility, fervency, faith, love, and perseverance,[11] and when with others, in a known tongue.[12]

4. Prayer is to be made for things lawful and for all sorts of men living or that shall live hereafter,[13] but not for the dead[14] nor for those of whom it may be known that they have sinned the sin unto death.[15]

5. The reading of the Scriptures;[16] preaching and hearing the Word of God;[17] teaching and admonishing one another in psalms, hymns, and spiritual songs, singing with grace in our hearts to the Lord;[18] as also the administration of baptism[19] and the Lord's Supper[20] are all parts of religious worship of God to be performed in obedience to Him with understanding, faith, reverence, and godly fear; moreover, solemn humiliation

---

8   Psalm 65:2; 95:1-7
9   John 14:13,14
10   Romans 8:26
11   1 John 5:14
12   1 Corinthians 14:16-17
13   1 Timothy 2:1-2; 2 Samuel 7:29
14   2 Samuel 12:21-23
15   1 John 5:16
16   1 Timothy 4:13
17   2 Timothy 4:2; Luke 8:18
18   Colossians 3:16; Ephesians 5:19
19   Matthew 28:19-20
20   1 Corinthians 11:26

with fastings[21] and thanksgiving upon special occasions ought to be used in a holy and religious manner.[22]

6. Neither prayer nor any other part of religious worship is now under the Gospel tied unto, or made more acceptable by, any place in which it is performed or toward which it is directed;[23] but God is to be worshipped everywhere in spirit and in truth; as in private families[24] daily[25] and in secret each one by himself,[26] so more solemnly in the public assemblies which are not carelessly nor willfully to be neglected or forsaken, when God by His word or providence calleth thereunto.[27]

7. As it is of the law of nature that, in general, a proportion of time by God's appointment be set apart for the worship of God, so by His Word in a positive, moral, and perpetual commandment, binding all men in all ages, He hath particularly appointed one day in seven to be kept holy unto Him,[28] which from the beginning of the world to the resurrection of Christ was the last day of the week, and from the resurrection of Christ was changed into the first day of the week, which is called the Lord's Day, and is to be continued to

---

21   Esther 4:16; Joel 2:12
22   Exodus 15:1; Psalm 107
23   John 4:21; Malachi 1:11; 1 Timothy 2:8
24   Acts 10:2
25   Matthew 6:11; Psalm 55:17
26   Matthew 6:6
27   Hebrews 10:25; Acts 2:42
28   Exodus 20:8

the end of the world, the observation of the last day of the week being abolished.[29]

8. This day is kept holy unto the Lord when men, after a due preparing of their hearts and ordering their common affairs aforehand, are taken up in the public and private exercises of His worship and in the duties of necessity and mercy.[30]

---

29   1 Corinthians 16:1-2; Acts 20:7; Revelation 1:10
30   Matthew 12:1-13

CHAPTER 23

LAWFUL OATHS AND VOWS

1. A lawful oath is a part of religious worship wherein the person swearing in truth, righteousness, and judgment solemnly calleth God to witness what he swears[1] and to judge him according to the truth or falseness thereof.[2]

2. The name of God only is that by which men ought to swear, and therein, it is to be used with all holy fear and reverence; therefore, to swear vainly or rashly by that glorious and dreadful name, or to swear at all by any other thing, is sinful and to be abhorred;[3] yet as in matters of weight and moment for confirmation of truth and ending all strife,[4] an oath is warranted by the Word of God; so a lawful oath being imposed by lawful authority in such matters ought to be taken.[5]

3. Whosoever taketh an oath warranted by the Word of God ought duly to consider the weightiness of so solemn an

---

1   Exodus 20:7; Deuteronomy 10:20; Jeremiah 4:2
2   2 Chronicles 6:22-23
3   Matthew 5:34, 37; James 5:12
4   Hebrews 6:16; 2 Corinthians 1:23
5   Nehemiah 13:25

act, and therein to avouch nothing but what he knows to be the truth, for that by rash, false, and vain oaths the Lord is provoked, and for them this land mourns.[6]

4. An oath is to be taken in the plain and common sense of the words, without equivocation or mental reservation.[7]

5. A vow, which is not to be made to any creature but to God alone, is to be made and performed with all religious care and faithfulness;[8] but popish, monastical vows of perpetual single life,[9] professed poverty,[10] and regular obedience are so far from being degrees of higher perfection that they are superstitious and sinful snares in which no Christian may entangle himself.[11]

---

6   Leviticus 19:12; Jeremiah 23:10
7   Psalm 24:4
8   Psalm 76:11; Genesis 28:20-22
9   1 Corinthians 7:2, 9
10   Ephesians 4:28
11   Matthew 19:11

CHAPTER 24

THE CIVIL MAGISTRATE

1. God, the supreme Lord and King of all the world, hath ordained civil magistrates to be under Him, over the people, for His own glory and the public good, and to this end, hath armed them with the power of the sword for defense and encouragement of them who do good and for the punishment of evildoers.[1]

2. It is lawful for Christians to accept and execute the office of a magistrate when called thereunto in the management whereof, as they ought especially to maintain justice and peace according to the wholesome laws of each kingdom and commonwealth;[2] so for that end, they may lawfully now under the New Testament wage war upon just and necessary occasions.[3]

3. Civil magistrates, being set up by God for the ends aforesaid, subjection in all lawful things commanded by them, ought to be yielded by us in the Lord, not only for wrath but

---

1   Romans 13:1-4
2   2 Samuel 23:3; Psalm 82:3-4
3   Luke 3:14

for conscience's sake;[4] and we ought to make supplications and prayers for kings and all who are in authority, that under them we may live a quiet and peaceable life in all godliness and honesty.[5]

---

4   Romans 13:5-7; 1 Peter 2:17
5   1 Timothy 2:1-2

CHAPTER 25

MARRIAGE

1. Marriage is to be between one man and one woman; neither is it lawful for any man to have more than one wife, nor for any woman to have more than one husband at the same time.[1]

2. Marriage was ordained for the mutual help of husband and wife,[2] for the increase of mankind with a legitimate issue,[3] and for the prevention of uncleanness.[4]

3. It is lawful for all sorts of people to marry, who are able with judgment to give their consent;[5] yet it is the duty of Christians to marry in the Lord,[6] and therefore, such as profess the true religion should not marry with infidels or idolaters; neither should such as are godly be unequally yoked by marrying with such as are wicked in their life or maintain damnable heresy.[7]

---

1   Genesis 2:24; Malachi 2:15; Matthew 19:5-6
2   Genesis 2:18
3   Genesis 1:28
4   1 Corinthians 7:2, 9
5   Hebrews 13:4; 1 Timothy 4:3
6   1 Corinthians 7:39
7   Nehemiah 13:25-27

4. Marriage ought not to be within the degrees of consanguinity or affinity forbidden in the Word;[8] nor can such incestuous marriage ever be made lawful by any law of man or consent of parties, so as those persons may live together as man and wife.[9]

---

8   Leviticus 18
9   Mark 6:18; 1 Corinthians 5:1

CHAPTER 26

THE CHURCH

1. The catholic or universal Church, which (with respect to the internal work of the Spirit and truth of grace) may be called invisible, consists of the whole number of Spirit-baptized believers that have been, are, or shall be gathered into one under Christ the Head thereof and is the spouse, the body, the fulness of Him Who fills all in all.[1]

2. All persons throughout the world professing the faith of the Gospel and obedience unto God by Christ, according unto it, not destroying their own profession by any errors everting the foundation, or unholiness of life, are and may be called visible saints;[2] and of such ought all particular congregations to be constituted.[3]

3. The purest churches under Heaven are subject to mixture and error,[4] and some have so degenerated as to become not churches of Christ but synagogues of Satan;[5] nevertheless,

---

1   Hebrews 12:23; Colossians 1:18; Ephesians 1:10, 22-23; 5:23, 27, 32
2   1 Corinthians 1:2; Acts 11:26
3   Romans 1:7; Ephesians 1:20-22
4   1 Corinthians 15; Revelation 2-3
5   Revelation 18:2; 2 Thessalonians 2:11-12

Christ always hath had and ever shall have a true Church in this world to the end thereof, of such as believe in Him and make profession of His name.[6]

4. The Lord Jesus Christ is the Head of the Church, in Whom by the appointment of the Father, all power for the calling, institution, order, or government of the Church is invested in a supreme and Sovereign manner.[7]

5. In the execution of this power wherewith He is so entrusted, the Lord Jesus calleth out of the world unto Himself, through the ministry of His Word, by His Spirit, those who are given unto Him by His Father[8] that they may walk before Him in all the ways of obedience,[9] which He prescribes to them in His Word. Those thus called He commands to walk together in particular societies, or churches, for their mutual edification and the due performance of that public worship which He requires of them in the Word.[10]

6. The members of these churches are saints by calling,[11] visibly manifesting and evidencing (in and by their profession and walking) their obedience unto that call of Christ, and do willingly consent to walk together according to the appointment of Christ, giving up themselves to the Lord and

6   Matthew 16:18
7   Colossians 1:18; Matthew 28:18-20; Ephesians 4:11-12
8   John 10:16; 12:32
9   Matthew 28:20
10   Matthew 18:15-20
11   Romans 1:7; 1 Corinthians 1:2

one to another by the will of God in professed subjection to the ordinances of the Gospel.[12]

7. To each of these churches thus gathered, according to His mind declared in His Word, He hath given all that power and authority which is any way needful for their carrying on that order in worship and discipline which He hath instituted for them to observe, with commands and rules for the due and right exerting and executing of that power.[13]

8. A particular church gathered and completely organized according to the mind of Christ consists of officers and members, and the officers appointed by Christ to be chosen and set apart by the church (so called and gathered) for the peculiar administration of ordinances and execution of power or duty, which He entrusts them with or calls them to, to be continued to the end of the world, are pastors or elders and deacons.[14]

9. The way appointed by Christ for the calling of any person fitted and gifted by the Holy Spirit unto the office of pastor or elder in a church is that he be chosen thereunto by the common suffrage of the church itself[15] and solemnly set apart by fasting and prayer, with imposition of hands of the eldership of the church,[16] if there be any before constituted

---

12   Acts 2:41-42; 5:13-14; 2 Corinthians 9:13
13   Matthew 18:17-18; 1 Corinthians 5:4-5, 13; 2 Corinthians 2:6-8
14   Acts 20:17, 28; Philippians 1:1
15   Acts 14:23
16   1 Timothy 4:14

therein, and of a deacon that he be chosen by the like suffrage and set apart by prayer and the like imposition of hands.[17]

10. The work of pastors being constantly to attend the service of Christ in His churches in the ministry of the Word and prayer, with watching for their souls as they that must give an account to Him[18] is incumbent on the churches to whom they minister not only to give them all due respect but also to communicate to them of all their good things according to their ability so they may have a comfortable supply[19] without being themselves entangled in secular affairs[20] and may also be capable of exercising hospitality toward others;[21] and this is required by the law of nature and by the express order of our Lord Jesus, Who hath ordained that they who preach the Gospel should live of the Gospel.[22]

11. Although it be incumbent on the pastors or elders of the churches to be instant in preaching the Word by way of office, yet the work of preaching the Word is not so peculiarly confined to them; but that others also gifted and fitted by the Holy Spirit for it, and approved and called by the church, may and ought to perform it.[23]

---

17   Acts 6:3, 5-6
18   Acts 6:4; Hebrews 13:17
19   1 Timothy 5:17-18; Galatians 6:6-7
20   2 Timothy 2:4
21   1 Timothy 3:2
22   1 Corinthians 9:6-14
23   Acts 11:19-21; 1 Peter 4:10-11

12. As all believers are bound to join themselves to particular churches when and where they have opportunity to do so, so all that are admitted unto the privileges of a church are also under the censures and government thereof, according to the rule of Christ.[24]

13. No church members upon any offence taken by them, having performed their duty required of them toward the person they are offended at, ought to disturb any church order or absent themselves from the assemblies of the church or administration of any ordinances upon the account of such offense at any of their fellow members, but to wait upon Christ in the further proceeding of the church.[25]

14. As each church and all the members of it are bound to pray continually for the good and prosperity of all the churches of Christ in all places[26] and upon all occasions to further it (every one within the bounds of their places and callings in the exercise of their gifts and graces) so the churches, when planted by the Providence of God so they may enjoy opportunity and advantage for it, ought to hold communion among themselves for their peace, increase of love, and mutual edification.[27]

---

24   1 Thessalonians 5:14; 2 Thessalonians 3:6, 14-15
25   Matthew 18:15-17; Ephesians 4:2-3
26   Ephesians 6:18
27   Romans 16:1-2; 3 John 8-10

15. In cases of difficulties or differences either in point of doctrine or administration, wherein either the churches in general are concerned, or any one church in their peace, union, and edification, or any member or members of any church are injured in or by any proceedings in censures not agreeable to truth and order, it is according to the mind of Christ that many churches holding communion together do, by their messengers, meet to consider and give their advice in or about that matter in difference to be reported to all the churches concerned;[28] howbeit, these messengers assembled are not entrusted with any church power properly so called or with any jurisdiction over the churches themselves to exercise any censures either over any churches or persons or to impose their determination on the churches or officers.[29]

---

28 Acts 15:2, 4, 6, 22-23, 25
29 2 Corinthians 1:24; 1 John 4:1

CHAPTER 27

THE COMMUNION OF SAINTS

1. All saints who are united to Jesus Christ their Head by His Spirit and faith, although they are not made thereby one person with Him, have fellowship in His graces, sufferings, death, resurrection, and glory;[1] and being united to one another in love, they have communion in each other's gifts and graces;[2] and are obliged to the performance of such duties, public and private, in an orderly way as do conduce to their mutual good, both in the inward and outward man.[3]

2. Saints, by profession, are bound to maintain a holy fellowship and communion in the worship of God and in performing such other spiritual services as tend to their mutual edification,[4] as also in relieving each other in outward things according to their several abilities and necessities,[5] which communion according to the rule of the Gospel, though especially to be exercised by them in the relations wherein

---

1   1 John 1:3; John 1:16; Philippians 3:10; Romans 6:5-6
2   Ephesians 4:15-16; 1 Corinthians 3:21-23; 12:7
3   1 Thessalonians 5:11, 14; Romans 1:12; 1 John 3:17-18; Galatians 6:10
4   Hebrews 10:24-25, 3:12-13
5   Acts 12:29-30

they stand, whether in families[6] or churches,[7] yet as God offers opportunity is to be extended to all the household of faith, even all those who in every place call upon the name of the Lord Jesus; nevertheless, their communion one with another as saints doth not take away or infringe the title or propriety which each man hath in his goods and possessions.[8]

---

6   Ephesians 6:4
7   1 Corinthians 12:14-27
8   Acts 5:4; Ephesians 4:28

CHAPTER 28

BAPTISM AND THE LORD'S SUPPER

1. Baptism and the Lord's Supper are ordinances of positive and Sovereign institution, appointed by the Lord Jesus, the only Lawgiver, to be continued in His Church to the end of the world.[1]

2. These holy appointments are to be administered only by those who are qualified and thereunto called according to the commission of Christ.[2]

---

1   Matthew 28:19-20; 1 Corinthians 11:26
2   Matthew 28:19; 1 Corinthians 4:1

CHAPTER 29

BAPTISM

1. Baptism is an ordinance of the New Testament, ordained by Jesus Christ, to be unto the party baptized a sign of his fellowship with Him in his death and resurrection,[1] of his being engrafted into Him, of remission of sins,[2] and of his giving up unto God through Jesus Christ to live and walk in newness of life.[3]

2. Those who do actually profess repentance toward God and faith in and obedience to our Lord Jesus are the only proper subjects of this ordinance.[4]

3. The outward element to be used in this ordinance is water, wherein the party is to be baptized in the name of the Father, and of the Son, and of the Holy Spirit.[5]

4. Immersion, or dipping of the person in water, is necessary to the due administration of this ordinance.[6]

---

1   Romans 6:3-5; Colossians 2:12; Galatians 3:27
2   Mark 1:4; Acts 26:16
3   Romans 6:2, 4
4   Mark 16:16; Acts 8:36-37
5   Matthew 28:19-20; Acts 8:38
6   Matthew 3:16; John 3:23

CHAPTER 30

THE LORD'S SUPPER

1. The Supper of the Lord Jesus was instituted by Him the same night wherein He was betrayed to be observed in His churches unto the end of the world for the perpetual remembrance and showing forth the sacrifice of Himself in His death, confirmation of the faith of believers in all the benefits thereof, their spiritual nourishment and growth in Him, their further engagement in and to all duties which they owe unto Him,[1] and to be a bond and pledge of their communion with Him and with each other.[2]

2. In this ordinance, Christ is not offered up to His Father nor any real sacrifice made at all for remission of sin of the quick or dead, but only a memorial of that One offering up of Himself, by Himself, upon the cross, once for all,[3] and a spiritual oblation of all possible praise unto God for the same, so that the popish sacrifice of the Mass (as they call it) is most

---

1   1 Corinthians 11:23-26
2   1 Corinthians 10:16-17, 21
3   Hebrews 9:25-26, 28

abominable, injurious to Christ's own only sacrifice, the alone propitiation for all the sins of the elect.[4]

3. The Lord Jesus hath, in this ordinance, appointed His ministers to pray and bless the elements of bread and wine and thereby to set them apart from a common to a holy use, and to take and break the bread, to take the cup, and (they communicating also themselves) to give both to the communicants.[5]

4. The denial of the cup to the people, worshipping the elements, lifting them up or carrying them about for adoration, and reserving them for any pretended religious use are all contrary to the nature of this ordinance and to the institution of Christ.[6]

5. The outward elements in this ordinance, duly set apart to the uses ordained by Christ, have such relation to Him crucified as that truly, although in terms used figuratively, they are sometimes called by the name of the things they represent, to wit the body and blood of Christ;[7] albeit in substance and nature, they still remain truly and only bread and wine as they were before.[8]

6. That doctrine which maintains a change of the substance of bread and wine into the substance of Christ's body and blood (commonly called transubstantiation) by

4   1 Corinthians 11:24; Matthew 26:26-27
5   1 Corinthians 11:23-26
6   Matthew 26:26-28, 15:9; Exodus 20:4-5
7   1 Corinthians 11:27
8   1 Corinthians 11:26, 28

consecration of a priest, or by any other way, is repugnant not to Scripture alone, but even to common sense and reason,[9] overthrows the nature of the ordinance, and hath been and is the cause of manifold superstitions, yea, of gross idolatries.[10]

7. Worthy receivers, outwardly partaking of the visible elements in this ordinance, do then inwardly by faith, not carnally and corporally, receive and feed upon Christ crucified and all the benefits of His death, the body and blood of Christ being not corporally or carnally present in the elements.[11]

8. All ignorant and ungodly persons, as they are unfit to enjoy communion with Christ,[12] so are they unworthy of the Lord's Table and cannot, without great sin against Him while they remain such, partake of these holy mysteries or be admitted thereunto; yea whosoever shall receive unworthily are guilty of the body and blood of the Lord, eating and drinking judgment to themselves.[13]

---

9   Acts 3:21; Luke 24:6, 39
10   1 Corinthians 11:24-25
11   1 Corinthians 10:16, 11:23-26
12   2 Corinthians 6:14-15
13   1 Corinthians 11:29; Matthew 7:6

CHAPTER 31

THE STATE OF MAN AFTER DEATH

1. The bodies of men after death return to dust and see corruption,[1] but their souls (which neither die nor sleep), having an immortal subsistence, immediately return to God Who gave them;[2] the souls of the righteous being then made perfect in holiness are received into paradise, where they are with Christ and behold the face of God in light and glory, waiting for the full redemption of their bodies;[3] and the souls of the wicked are cast into Hell, where they remain in torment and utter darkness, reserved to the judgment of the Great Day;[4] besides these two places for souls separated from their bodies, the Scripture acknowledges none.

---

1   Genesis 3:19; Acts 13:36
2   Ecclesiastes 12:7
3   Luke 23:43; 2 Corinthians 5:1, 6, 8; Philippians 1:23; Hebrews 12:23
4   Judges 6:7; 1 Peter 3:19; Luke 16:23-24

CHAPTER 32

THE LAST JUDGMENTS

1. God hath appointed a day wherein He will judge the world in righteousness by Jesus Christ,[1] to Whom all power and judgment is given of the Father, in which day not only the apostate angels shall be judged, but likewise, all persons who have lived upon the earth shall appear before the tribunal of Christ[2] to give an account of their thoughts, words, and deeds, and to receive according to what they have done in the body, whether good or evil.[3]

2. On that day, Christ will first remove His Church from the earth by resurrection and translation;[4] then pour out God's righteous judgments on the world of unbelief;[5] afterward descend with His Church and establish His glorious kingdom over all nations for a thousand years,[6] at the close of which He will raise the unrighteous dead for their final

---

1   Acts 17:31; John 5:22, 27
2   1 Corinthians 6:3; Judges 6
3   2 Corinthians 5:10; Ecclesiastes 12:14; Matthew 12:36; 25:32; Romans 14:10, 12
4   John 14:1-3; 1 Thessalonians 4:13-18; Revelation 3:10
5   Matthew 25:31-46; Mark 13; Revelation 5-19
6   Revelation 19:11-20:6

judgment and usher His saints into the everlasting kingdom of His Father in a new heaven and new earth.[7]

3. The end of God's appointing these judgments is for the manifestation of the glory of His mercy in the eternal salvation of the elect[8] and of His justice in the eternal damnation of the reprobate, who are wicked and disobedient.[9]

4. As Christ would have us to be certainly persuaded that there shall be a Day of Judgment, both to deter all men from sin[10] and for the greater consolation of the godly in their adversity,[11] so will He have that day unknown to men, that they may shake off all carnal security and be always watchful because they know not at what hour the Lord will come[12] and may ever be prepared to say, "Come, Lord Jesus, come quickly." Amen.[13]

---

7   1 Corinthians 15:24-28; Revelation 20:7-22:19
8   Matthew 25:21, 34; 2 Timothy 4:8
9   Matthew 25:46; Mark 9:48; 2 Thessalonians 1:7-10
10   2 Corinthians 5:10-11
11   2 Thessalonians 1:5-7
12   Mark 13:35-37; Luke 13:35-36
13   Revelation 22:20

APPENDIX ON BAPTISM

Whosoever reads and impartially considers what we have declared in our foregoing confession may readily perceive that we do not only consent with all other true Christians on the Word of God (revealed in the Scriptures of truth) as the foundation and rule of our faith and worship but that we have also industriously endeavored to manifest that in the fundamental Articles of Christianity we mind the same things and have therefore expressed our belief in the same words that have on the like occasion been spoken by other societies of Christians before us.

This we have done that those who are desirous to know the principles of religion which we hold and practice may take an estimate from ourselves (who jointly concur in this work) and may not be misguided, either by undue reports or by the ignorance or errors of particular persons, who going under the same name with ourselves may give an occasion of scandalizing the truth we profess.

And although we do differ from our brethren who are Paedobaptists in the subject and administration of baptism, and such other circumstances as have a necessary dependence on our observance of that ordinance, and do frequent our own assemblies for our mutual edification, and discharge of those duties and services which we owe unto God, and in His fear to each other, yet we would not be from hence misconstrued, as if the discharge of our own consciences herein did any ways disoblige or alienate our affections, or conversation from any others that fear the Lord, but that we may and do as we have opportunity participate of the labors of those whom God hath indued with abilities above ourselves, and qualified, and called to the ministry of the Word, earnestly desiring to approve ourselves to be such as follow after peace with holiness, and therefore, we always keep that blessed irenicism, or healing Word of the Apostle before our eyes; if in anything ye be otherwise minded, God shall reveal even this unto you; nevertheless, whereto we have already attained, let us walk by the same rule, let us mind the same thing (Philippians 3:15-16).

Let it not therefore be judged of us (because much hath been written on this subject, and yet we continue this our practice different from others) that it is out of obstinacy, but rather as the truth is that we do herein, according to the best of our understandings, worship God out of a pure mind, yielding obedience to His precept, in that method which we take to be most agreeable to the Scriptures of truth and primitive practice.

It would not become us to give any such intimation as should carry a semblance that what we do in the service of God is with a doubting conscience or with any such temper of mind that we do thus for the present with a reservation that we will do otherwise hereafter upon more mature deliberation; nor have we any cause to do so, being fully persuaded that what we do is agreeable to the will of God. Yet we do heartily propose this, that if any of the servants of our Lord Jesus shall, in the spirit of meekness, attempt to convince us of any mistake either in judgment or practice, we shall diligently ponder his arguments and accompt him our chiefest friend who shall be an instrument to convert us from any error that is in our ways, for we cannot wittingly do anything against the truth, but all things for the truth.

And therefore, we have endeavored seriously to consider what hath been already offered for our satisfaction in this point, and are loath to say any more, lest we be esteemed desirous of renewed contests thereabout; yet forasmuch as it may justly be expected that we show some reason why we cannot acquiesce in what hath been urged against us, we shall, with as much brevity as may consist with plainness, endeavor to satisfy the expectation of those who shall peruse what we now publish in this matter also.

1. As to those Christians who consent with us that repentance from dead works and faith toward God and our

Lord Jesus Christ is required in persons to be baptized and do, therefore, supply the defect of the infant, being uncapable of making confession of either, by others who do undertake these things for it, although we do find by church history that this hath been a very antient practice, yet considering that the same Scripture which does caution us against censuring our brother, with whom we shall all stand before the judgment seat of Christ, does also instruct us that every one of us shall give an account of himself to God, and whatsoever is not of faith is sin (Romans 14:4, 10, 12, 23). Therefore, we cannot for our own parts be persuaded in our own minds to build such a practice as this upon an unwritten tradition, but do rather choose in all points of faith and worship to have recourse to the holy Scriptures for the information of our judgment and regulation of our practice, being well-assured that a conscientious attending thereto is the best way to prevent and rectify our defects and errors (2 Timothy 3:16-17). And if any such case happens to be debated between Christians which is not plainly determinable by the Scriptures, we think it safest to leave such things undecided until the second coming of our Lord Jesus, as they did in the Church of old, until there should arise a Priest with Urim and Thummim Who might certainly inform them of the mind of God thereabout (Ezra 2:62-63).

2. As for those our Christian brethren who do ground their arguments for infants' baptism upon a presumed

federal holiness, or church membership, we conceive they are deficient in this, that albeit this covenant holiness and membership should be as is supposed in reference unto the infants of believers, yet no command for infant baptism does immediately and directly result from such a quality or relation.

All instituted worship receives its sanction from the precept and is to be thereby governed in all the necessary circumstances thereof.

So it was in the covenant that God made with Abraham and his seed. The sign whereof was appropriated only to the male, notwithstanding that the female seed, as well as the male, were comprehended in the covenant and part of the people of God; neither was this sign to be affixed to any male infant till he was eight days old; albeit, he was within the covenant from the first moment of his life; nor could the danger of death, or any other supposed necessity, warrant the circumcising of him before the set time, nor was there any cause for it; the threat of being cut off from his people, being only upon the neglect or contempt of the precept.

Righteous Lot was nearly related to Abraham in the flesh and contemporary with him when this covenant was made; yet inasmuch as he did not descend from his loins, nor was of his household family (although he was of the same household of faith with Abraham) yet neither Lot himself nor any of his posterity (because of their descent from him) were signed with the signature of this covenant that was made with Abraham and his seed.

This may suffice to show that where there was both an express covenant and a sign thereof (such a covenant as did separate the persons with whom it was made, and all their offspring from all the rest of the world, as a people holy unto the Lord, and did constitute them the visible people of God, though not comprehensive of all the faithful in the world), yet the sign of this covenant was not affixed to all the persons who were within this covenant, nor to any of them till the prescribed season, nor to other faithful servants of God who were not of descent from Abraham. And consequently, that it depends purely upon the will of the Lawgiver to determine what shall be the sign of His covenant, unto whom, at what season, and upon what terms it shall be affixed.

If our brethren do suppose baptism to be the seal of the covenant which God makes with every believer (of which the Scriptures are altogether silent), it is not our concern to contend with them herein; yet we conceive the seal of that covenant is the indwelling of the Spirit of Christ in the particular and individual persons in whom He resides, and nothing else, neither do they or we suppose that baptism is in any such manner substituted in the place of circumcision as to have the same (and no other) latitude, extent, or terms than circumcision had; for that was it suited only for the male children, baptism is an ordinance suited for every believer, whether male or female. That extended to all the males who were born in Abraham's house, or bought with his money, equally with the males who proceeded from his own loins; but baptism is not so far extended in any true Christian Church that we know of, as to be administered to all the poor, infidel servants that the members thereof purchase for their service and introduce into their families, nor to the children born of them in their house.

But we conceive the same parity of reasoning may hold for the ordinance of baptism as for that of circumcision (Exodus 12:49), *viz,* one law for the stranger, as for the home born. If any desire to be admitted to all the ordinances and privileges of God's house, the door is open upon the same terms that any one person was ever admitted to all or any of those privileges that belong to the Christian Church; may all persons of right challenge the like admission.

As for that text of Scripture, it is Romans 4:11. He received circumcision, a seal of the righteousness of the faith which he had yet being uncircumcised; we conceive if the apostles' scope in that place be duly attended to, it will appear that no argument can be taken from thence to enforce infant baptism; and forasmuch as we find a full and fair account of those words given by the learned Dr. Lightfoot (a man not to be suspected of partiality in this controversy) in his *Hor. Hebrai* on 1 Corinthians 7:19, pages forty-two and forty-three, we shall transcribe his words at large, without any comment of our own upon them.

> Circumcision is nothing, if we respect the time, for now it was without use, that end of it being especially fulfilled; for which it had been instituted: this end the apostle declares in these words, Rom. 4:11. But I fear that by most translations they are not sufficiently suited to the end of circumcision, and the scope of the Apostle whilst something of their own is by them inserted.

And after the Doctor hath represented diverse versions of the words agreeing for the most part in sense with that which we have in our Bibles, he thus proceeds.

> Other versions are to the same purpose; as if circumcision was given to Abraham for a seal of that righteousness which he had being yet uncircumcised, which we will not deny to be in some sense true, but we believe that circumcision had chiefly a far different respect.

> Give me leave thus to render the words; And he received the sign of circumcision, a seal of the righteousness of faith, which was to be in the uncircumcision, which was to be (I say) not which had been, not that which Abraham had whilst he was yet uncircumcised; but that which his uncircumcised seed should have, that is the

Gentiles, who in time to come should imitate the faith of Abraham.

Now consider well on what occasion circumcision was instituted unto Abraham, setting before thine eyes the history thereof, Gen. 17.

This promise is first made unto him, thou shalt be the father of many nations (in what sense the apostle explains in that chapter) and then there is subjoined a double seal for the confirmation of the thing, to wit, the change of the name Abram into Abraham, and the institution of circumcision, v. 4. Behold as for me, my covenant is with thee, and thou shalt be the father of many nations. Wherefore was his name called Abraham for the sealing of this promise. Thou shalt be the father of many nations. And wherefore was circumcision instituted to him? For the sealing of the same promise. Thou shalt be the father of many nations. So that this is the sense of the apostle; most agreeable to the institution of circumcision; he received the sign of circumcision, a seal of the righteousness of faith which in time to come the uncircumcision (or the Gentiles) should have and obtain.

Abraham had a twofold seed, natural, of the Jews; and faithful, of the believing Gentiles:

his natural seed was signed with the sign of circumcision, first indeed for the distinguishing of them from all other nations whilst they as yet were not the seed of Abraham, but especially for the memorial of the justification of the Gentiles by faith, when at length they should become his seed. Therefore, circumcision was of right to cease, when the Gentiles were brought into the faith, forasmuch as then it had obtained its last and chief end, and thenceforth circumcision is nothing.

Thus far he, which we earnestly desire may be seriously weighed, for we plead not his authority, but the evidence of truth in his words.

3. Of whatsoever nature the holiness of the children mentioned (1 Corinthians 7:12) be, yet they who do conclude that all such children (whether infants or of riper years) have from hence an immediate right to baptism, do as we conceive put more into the conclusion than will be found in the premises.

For although we do not determine positively concerning the apostle's scope in the holiness here mentioned, so as to say it is this or that and no other thing, yet it is evident that the apostle does by it determine not only the lawfulness but the expedience also of a believer's cohabitation with an unbeliever in the state of marriage.

And we do think that although the apostle's asserting of the unbelieving yokefellow to be sanctified by the believer should carry in it somewhat more than is in the bare marriage of two infidels because although the marriage covenant has a Divine sanction so as to make the wedlock of two unbelievers a lawful action, and their conjunction and cohabitation in that respect undefiled, yet there might be no ground to suppose from thence that both or either of their persons are thereby sanctified; and the apostle urges the cohabitation of a believer with an infidel in the state of wedlock from this ground that the unbelieving husband is sanctified by the believing wife; nevertheless, here you have the influence of a believer's faith ascending from an inferior to a superior relation, from the wife to the husband, who is her head, before it can descend to their offspring. And therefore we say, whatever be the nature or extent of the holiness here intended, we conceive it cannot convey to the children an immediate right to baptism because it would then be of another nature and of a larger extent than the root, and original from whence it is derived, for it is clear by the apostle's argument that holiness cannot be derived to the child from the sanctity of one parent only; if either father or mother be (in the sense intended by the apostle) unholy or unclean, so will the child be also; therefore, for the production of a holy seed, it is necessary that both of the parents be sanctified; and this the apostle positively asserts in the first place to be done by the believing parent, although the other be an unbeliever, and then consequentially, from thence argues, the holiness of their children. Hence it follows, that as the children have no other holiness than what they derive from both their parents, so neither can they have any right by this holiness to any spiritual privilege but such as both their parents did also partake of, and therefore, if the unbelieving parent (though sanctified by the believing parent) have not thereby a right to baptism, neither can we conceive that there is any such privilege derived to the children by their birth holiness.

Besides, if it had been the usual practice in the apostles' days for the father or mother who did believe to bring all their children with them to be baptized, then the holiness of the believing Corinthian's children would not at all have been in question when this epistle was written but might have been argued from their passing under that ordinance, which represented their new birth, although they had derived no holiness from their parents by their first birth and would have lain as an exception against the apostle's inference, else were your children unclean, etc. But of the sanctification of all the children of every believer by this ordinance, or any other way than what is beforementioned, the Scripture is altogether silent.

This may also be added, that if this birth holiness does qualify all the children of every believer for the ordinance of baptism, why not for all other ordinances? Why not for the Lord's Supper as was practiced for a long time together? For if recourse be had to what the Scriptures speak generally of this subject, it will be found that the same qualities which do entitle any person to baptism do so also for the participation of all the ordinances and privileges of the house of God that are common to all believers.

Whosoever can and does interrogate his good conscience toward God when he is baptized (as everyone must do who makes it to himself a sign of salvation) is capable of doing the same thing in every other act of worship that he performs.

4. The arguments and inferences that are usually brought for or against infant baptism from those few instances which the Scriptures afford us of whole families being baptized are only conjectural, and therefore, cannot of themselves be conclusive on either hand; yet in regard, most who treat on this subject for infant baptism do (as they conceive) improve these instances to the advantage of their argument. We think it fitting (in like manner as in the cases beforementioned, so in this) to show the invalidity of such inferences.

Cornelius worshipped God with all his house. The jailor and Crispus, the chief ruler of the synagogue, believed God with each of their houses. The household of Stephanus addicted themselves to the ministry of the saints, so that thus far, worshipping and believing runs parallel with baptism.

And if Lydia had been a married person when she believed, it is probable her husband would also have been named by the apostle, as in like cases, inasmuch as he would have been not only a part, but also the head of that baptized household.

Who can assign any probable reason why the apostle should make mention of four or five households being baptized and no more? Or why does he so often vary in the method of his salutations (Romans 1:6), sometimes mentioning only particular persons of great note, other times such, "and the Church in their house," meaning the saints who were with them and belonging to Narcissus who were in the Lord—thus saluting either whole families, or part of families, or only particular persons in families, considered as they were in the Lord; for if it had been a usual practice to baptize all children with their parents. There were then many thousands of the Jews who believed and a great number of the Gentiles in most of the principal cities in the world; and among so many thousands, it is more than probable there would have been some thousands of households baptized. Why then should the apostle, in this respect, signalize one family of the Jews and three or four of the Gentiles as particular instances in a case that was common? Whoever supposes that we do willfully debar our children from the benefit of any promise or privilege that of right belongs to the children of believing parents, they do entertain over severe thoughts of us. To be without natural affections is one of the characteristics of the worst of persons, in the worst of times. We do freely confess ourselves guilty before the Lord, in that we have not with more circumspection and diligence trained up those who relate to us in the fear of the Lord, and do humbly and earnestly pray that our omissions herein may be remitted, and that they may not redound to the prejudice of ourselves, or any of ours, but with respect to that duty that is incumbent on us, we acknowledge ourselves obliged by the precepts of God to bring up our children in the nurture and admonition of the Lord, to teach them His fear, both by instruction and example. And should we set light by this precept, it would demonstrate that we are more vile than the unnatural heathen who like not to retain God in their knowledge. Our baptism might then be justly accompted as no baptism to us.

There are many special promises that do encourage us, as well as precepts that do oblige us to the close pursuit of our duty herein: that God Whom we serve, being jealous of His worship, threatens the visiting of the father's transgression upon the children to the third and fourth generation of them who hate Him, yet does more abundantly extend His mercy, even to thousands (respecting the offspring and succeeding generations) of them who love Him and keep His commands.

Our Lord rebuked His disciples for prohibiting the access of little children who were brought to Him that He might pray over them, lay His hands upon them, and bless them, declaring that of such is the Kingdom of God. And the apostle Peter, in answer to their inquiry that desired to know what they must do to be saved, does not only instruct them in the necessary duty of repentance and baptism, but does also thereto encourage them by that promise which had reference both to them and their children; if our Lord Jesus in the forementioned place does not respect the qualities of children (as elsewhere) as to their meekness, humility, sincerity, and the like, but intend also that those very persons and such like appertain to the Kingdom of God, and if the apostle Peter, in mentioning the aforesaid promise, does respect not only the present and succeeding generations of those Jews who heard him (in which sense the same phrase doth occur in Scripture), but also the immediate offspring of his auditors, whether the promise relates to the gift of the Holy Spirit, or of eternal life, or any grace, or privilege tending to the obtaining thereof, it is neither our concern nor our interest to confine the mercies and promises of God to a more narrow or less compass than He is pleased gratuitously to offer and intend them; nor to have a light esteem of them, but are obliged in duty to God and affection to our children to plead earnestly with God and use our utmost endeavors that both ourselves and our offspring may be partakers of His mercies and gracious promises: yet we cannot from either of these texts collect a sufficient warrant for us to baptize our children before they are instructed in the principles of the Christian religion.

For as to the instance in little children, it seems by the disciples forbidding them that they were brought upon some other account, not so frequent as baptism must be supposed to have been, if from the beginning, believers' children had been admitted thereto, and no account is given whether their parents were baptized believers or not; and as to the instance of the apostle, if the following words and practices may be taken as an interpretation of the scope of that promise, we cannot conceive it does refer to infant baptism, because the text does presently subjoin, "Then they that gladly received the word were baptized."

That there were some believing children of believing parents in the apostles' days is evident from the Scriptures, even such as were then in their father's family and under their parents' tuition and education to whom the apostle, in several of his epistles to the churches, giveth commands to obey their parents in the Lord and does allure their tender years to hearken to this precept, by reminding them that it is the first command with promise.

And it is recorded by him for the praise of Timothy and encouragement of parents betimes to instruct and children early to attend to godly instruction, that from a child, he had known the holy Scriptures.

The apostle John rejoiced greatly when he found the children of the Elect Lady walking in the truth, and the children of her Elect Sister joined with the apostle in his salutation.

But that this was not generally so, that all the children of believers were accounted for believers (as they would have been if they had all been baptized) may be collected from the character which the apostle gives of persons fit to be chosen to eldership in the church, which was not common to all believers; among others, this is expressly one, *viz*, if there be any having believing or faithful children, not accused of riot or unruly; and we may from the apostles' writings on the same subject collect the reason of this qualification, *viz*, that in case the person designed for this office to teach and rule in the house of God had children capable of it, there might be first a proof of his ability, industry, and success in this work in his own family and private capacity before he was ordained to the exercise of this authority in the church, in a public capacity, as a bishop in the house of God.

These things we have mentioned as having a direct reference unto the controversy between our brethren and us; other things that are more abstruse and prolix, which are frequently introduced into this controversy, but do not necessarily concern it, we have purposely avoided that the distance between us and our brethren may not be by us made more wide; for it is our duty and concern so far as is possible for us (retaining a good conscience toward God) to seek a more entire agreement and reconciliation with them.

We are not insensible that as to the order of God's house and entire communion therein, there are some things wherein we (as well as others) are not at a full accord among ourselves, as for instance, the known principle and state of the consciences of diverse of us, who have agreed in this Confession is such; that we cannot hold church communion with any other than baptized believers and churches constituted of such; yet some others of us have a greater liberty and freedom in our spirits that way; and therefore, we have purposely omitted the mention of things of that nature that we might concur with in giving this evidence of our agreement, both among ourselves and with other good Christians in those important articles of the Christian religion mainly insisted on by us: and this notwithstanding, we all esteem it our chief concern, both among ourselves and all others who in every place call upon the name of the Lord Jesus Christ our Lord, both theirs and ours, and love Him in sincerity, to endeavor to keep the unity of the Spirit in the bond of peace and in order thereunto, to exercise all lowliness and meekness, with longsuffering, forbearing one another in love.

And we are persuaded if the same method were introduced into frequent practice between us and our Christian friends who agree with us in all the fundamental articles of the

Christian faith (though they do not so in the subject and administration of baptism), it would soon beget a better understanding and brotherly affection between us.

In the beginning of the Christian Church, when the doctrine of the baptism of Christ was not universally understood, those who knew only the baptism of John were the disciples of the Lord Jesus and Apollos, an eminent minister of the Gospel of Jesus.

In the beginning of the reformation and recovery from that Egyptian darkness wherein our forefathers for many generations were held in bondage, upon recourse had to the Scriptures of truth, different apprehensions were conceived, which are to this time continued, concerning the practice of this ordinance.

Let not our zeal herein be misinterpreted: that God Whom we serve is jealous of His worship. By His gracious Providence, the Law thereof is continued among us; and we are forewarned by what happened among the Jews, that it is necessary for every generation, and that frequently, in every generation to consult the Divine oracle, compare our worship with the rule, and take heed to what doctrines we receive and practice.

If the ten commands exhibited in the popish idolatrous service books had been received as the entire law of God because they agree in number with his ten commands, and also in the substance of nine of them, the second commandment forbidding idolatry had been utterly lost.

If Ezra and Nehemiah had not made a diligent search into the particular parts of God's law and His worship, the Feast of Tabernacles (which for many centuries had not been duly observed, according to the institution, though it was retained in the general notion) would not have been kept in due order.

So may it be now as to many things relating to the service of God, which do retain the names proper to them in their first institution, but yet through inadvertency (where there is no sinister design) may vary in their circumstances from their first institution. And if by means of any antient defection, or of that general corruption of the service of God, and interruption of His true worship, and persecution of His servants by the antichristian Bishop of Rome, for many generations; those who do consult the Word of God cannot yet arrive at a full and mutual satisfaction among themselves what was the practice of the primitive Christian Church in some points relating to the worship of God: yet inasmuch as these things are not of the essence of Christianity, but that we agree in the fundamental doctrines thereof, we do apprehend there is sufficient ground to lay aside all bitterness and prejudice, and in the spirit of love and meekness embrace and own each other therein; leaving each other at liberty to

perform such other services (wherein we cannot concur) apart
unto God, according to the best of our understanding.

FINIS

INTRODUCTION TO
THE BAPTIST CATECHISM

A catechism is a confession of faith by another method. It teaches the basics of the faith by means of questions and answers, rather than by purely didactic propositions. Catechisms have a rich history in the Christian tradition, tracing back at least as far as Augustine of Hippo, John Chrysostom, and Cyril of Jerusalem. They were produced throughout the Middle Ages as well, though the term "catechism" itself was not used to describe them until the sixteenth century.

After the Protestant Reformation, the work of producing catechisms became a matter of urgent importance as Protestants and Catholics alike sought to hold on to their gains through these teaching tools. On both sides, the new catechisms relied heavily upon their medieval predecessors, and like them, were generally organized under the headings of Faith (Apostles' Creed), Hope (Lord's Prayer), and Love (Ten Commandments).

Just four years after adopting *The Baptist Confession of Faith* in 1693, the Particular Baptists of Great Britain determined that they, too, should have a catechism. They selected William

Collins, who had been instrumental in producing *The Baptist Confession*, to draft it for them.

Once again, Collins turned to the Presbyterians for his template. He drew heavily from their *Shorter Catechism* in both language and organization, making only minor changes to bring his work into line with Baptist distinctives. The finished product was published the same year it was commissioned, and it was a huge success. By 1695, it was already in its fifth edition.

This new edition of *The Baptist Catechism* preserves the substance of the original, with only minor changes to bring it into alignment with dispensational thought. For example, knowledgeable readers will notice that questions on the Ten Commandments have been slightly altered from their original wording. Whereas the original catechism asks, "What does the *Xth* commandment require/forbid?," it now reads, "What can we learn from the *Xth* commandment?" Dispensational Christians revere the Ten Commandments, as they do the rest of Scripture. But we also believe that the Mosaic Law was an indivisible unity. Thus, when the Old Covenant came to an end, we believe the Ten Commandments *as the Ten Commandments* also ceased to function as a rule of life for God's people. Yet the timeless moral truths embedded within those commandments remain, and these must be taught.

The astute reader may notice other minuscule changes as well, like updates to the spelling and capitalization of words. But throughout, I have endeavored to produce a catechism that still very much reads like the original. May the Lord use this new edition of *The Baptist Catechism* to ground many people in the faith, both within their local churches and around their hearths at home.

BRANDON CRAWFORD

Marshall, Michigan

Reformation Day 2021

THE BAPTIST CATECHISM

1. Q. Who is the first and chiefest being?

A. God is the first and chiefest being (Isaiah 44:6; 48:12; Psalm 97:9).

2. Q. Ought everyone to believe there is a God?

A. Everyone ought to believe there is a God (Hebrews 11:6), and it is their great sin and folly who do not (Psalm 14:1).

3. Q. How may we know there is a God?

A. The light of nature in man and the works of God plainly declare there is a God (Romans 1:19-20; Psalm 19:1-3; Acts 17:24), but His Word and Spirit only do it fully and effectually for the salvation of sinners (1 Corinthians 2:10; 2 Timothy 3:15-16).

4. Q. What is the Word of God?

A. The holy Scriptures of the Old and New Testament are the Word of God, and the only certain rule of faith and obedience (2 Timothy 3:16; Ephesians 2:20).

5. Q. May all men make use of the holy Scriptures?

A. All men are not only permitted but also commanded and exhorted to read, hear, and understand the holy Scriptures (John 5:38; 17:17,18; Revelation 1:3; Acts 8:30).

6. Q. What things are chiefly contained in the holy Scriptures?

A. The holy Scriptures chiefly contain what man ought to believe concerning God and what duty God requireth of man (2 Timothy 1:13; 3:15-16).

7. Q. What is God?

A. God is a Spirit (John 4:24), infinite (Job 11:7-9), eternal (Psalm 110:2), and unchangeable (James 1:17) in His being (Exodus 3:14), wisdom (Psalm 147:5), power (Revelation 4:8), holiness (Revelation 15:4), justice, goodness, and truth (Exodus 34:6).

8. Q. Are there more gods than one?

A. There is but one only, the living and true God (Deuteronomy 6:4; Jeremiah 10:10).

9. Q. How many Persons are there in the Godhead?

A. There are three Persons in the Godhead—the Father, the Son, and the Holy Spirit—and these three are one God, the same in essence, equal in power and glory (1 John 5:7; Matthew 28:19).

10. Q. What are the decrees of God?

A. The decrees of God are His eternal purpose according to the counsel of His will, whereby, for His own glory, He hath foreordained whatsoever comes to pass (Ephesians 1:4, 11; Romans 9:22-23; Isaiah 46:10; Lamentations 3:37).

11. Q. How doth God execute His decrees?

A. God executes His decrees in the works of creation and providence.

12. Q. What is the work of creation?

A. The work of creation is God making all things of nothing, by the word of His power, in the space of six days, and all very good (Genesis 1; Hebrews 11:3).

13. Q. How did God create man?

A. God created man, male and female, after His own image in knowledge, righteousness, and holiness with dominion over the creatures (Genesis 1:26-28; Colossians 3:10; Ephesians 4:24).

14. Q. What are God's works of Providence?

A. God's works of Providence are His most holy (Psalm 145:17), wise (Isaiah 28:29; Psalm 104:24), and powerful preserving (Hebrews 1:3) and governing all His creatures and all their actions (Psalm 103:19; Matthew 10:29-31).

15. Q. What special act of Providence did God exercise toward man in the state wherein he was created?

A. When God had created man, He promised life with him upon condition of perfect obedience, forbidding him to eat of the tree of the knowledge of good and evil upon pain of death (Galatians 3:12; Genesis 2:17).

16. Q. Did our first parents continue in the state wherein they were created?

A. Our first parents, being left to the freedom of their own will, fell from the estate wherein they were created by sinning against God (Genesis 3:6-8, 13; Ecclesiastes 7:29).

17. Q. What is sin?

A. Sin is any want of conformity unto, or transgression of, the law of God (1 John 3:4).

18. Q. What was the sin whereby our first parents fell from the state wherein they were created?

A. The sin whereby our first parents fell from the state wherein they were created was their eating the forbidden fruit (Genesis 3:6, 12, 16-17).

19. Q. Did all mankind fall in Adam's first transgression?

A. Adam stood not only for himself but for his posterity. Therefore, all mankind descending from him by ordinary generation sinned in him and fell with him in his first transgression (Genesis 2:16-17; Romans 5:12; 1 Corinthians 15:21-22).

20. Q. Into what state did the fall bring mankind?

A. The fall brought mankind into a state of sin and misery (Romans 5:12).

21. Q. Wherein consists the sinfulness of that state whereinto man fell?

A. The sinfulness of that state whereinto man fell consists in the guilt of Adam's first sin, the want of original righteousness, and the corruption of his whole nature, which is commonly called original sin, together with all actual transgressions which proceed from it (Romans 5:12-21; Ephesians 2:1-3; James 1:14-15; Matthew 15:19).

22. Q. What is the misery of that state whereinto man fell?

A. All mankind, by their fall, lost communion with God (Genesis 3:8, 10, 24), are under His wrath and curse (Ephesians 2:2-3; Galatians 3:10), and so made liable to all miseries in this life, to death itself, and to the pains of hell forever (Lamentations 3:39; Romans 6:23; Matthew 25:41, 46).

23. Q. Did God leave all mankind to perish in the state of sin and misery?

A. God, out of His good pleasure and grace, from all eternity, elected some to receive everlasting life (Ephesians 1:4-5), to deliver them out of the state of sin and misery, and to bring them into an estate of salvation by a Redeemer (Romans 3:20-22; Galatians 3:21-22).

24. Q. Who is the Redeemer of God's elect?

A. The only Redeemer of God's elect is the Lord Jesus Christ (1 Timothy 2:5, 6), Who, being the eternal Son of God, became man (John 1:14; Galatians 4:4), and so was and continues to be God and man in two distinct natures, and one Person, forever (Romans 9:5; Luke 1:35; Colossians 2:9; Hebrews 7:24-25).

25. Q. How did Christ, being the Son of God, become man?

A. Christ the Son of God became man by taking to Himself a true body (Hebrews 2:14, 17; 10:5) and a reasonable soul (Matthew 26:38), being conceived by the power of the Holy Spirit in the womb of the virgin Mary, and born of her (Luke 1:27, 31, 34-35, 42; Galatians 4:4), yet without sin (Hebrews 4:15, 7:26).

26. Q. What offices doth Christ execute as our Redeemer?

A. Christ, as our Redeemer, executes the offices of a prophet, of a priest, and of a king, both in His state of humiliation and exaltation (Acts 3:22; Hebrews 12:25; 2 Corinthians 13:3; Hebrews 5:5-7; 7:25; Psalm 2:6; Isaiah 9:6, 7; Matthew 21:5; Psalm 2:8-11).

27. Q. How doth Christ execute the office of a prophet?

A. Christ executes the office of prophet in revealing to us, by His Word and Spirit, the will of God for our salvation (John 1:18; 1 Peter 1:10-12; John 15:15; 20:31).

28. Q. How doth Christ execute the office of a priest?

A. Christ executes the office of priest in His once offering up Himself a sacrifice to satisfy Divine justice (Hebrews 9:14, 28) and reconcile us to God (Hebrews 2:17) and in making continual intercession for us (Hebrews 7:24-25).

29. Q. How doth Christ execute the office of king?

A. Christ executes the office of a king in subduing us to Himself (Acts 15:14-16), in ruling (Isaiah 33:22) and defending us (Isaiah 32:1-2), and in restraining and conquering all His and our enemies (1 Corinthians 15:25; Psalm 110).

30. Q. Of what did Christ's humiliation consist?

A. Christ's humiliation consisted in His being born and in a low condition (Luke 2:7), made under the law (Galatians 4:4), undergoing the miseries of this life (Hebrews 12:2-3; Isaiah 53:2-3), the wrath of God (Luke 22:44; Matthew 27:46), and the cursed death of the cross (Philippians 2:8); in being buried (1 Corinthians 15:3-4), and continuing under the power of death for a time (Acts 2:24-27, 31; Matthew 12:40).

31. Q. Of what did Christ's exaltation consist?

A. Christ's exaltation consists in His rising again from the dead on the third day (1 Corinthians 15:4), in ascending into Heaven (Mark 16:19), in sitting at the right hand of God the Father (Ephesians 1:20), and in coming to judge the world at the last day (Acts 1: 11; 17:31).

32. Q. How are we made partakers of the redemption purchased by Christ?

A. We are made partakers of the redemption purchased by Christ by the effectual application of it to us (John 1:11-12) by His Holy Spirit (Titus 3:5-6).

33. Q. How doth the Spirit apply to us the redemption purchased by Christ?

A. The Spirit applies to us the redemption purchased by Christ by working faith in us

(Ephesians 1:13-14; John 6:37, 39; Ephesians 2:8), and thereby uniting us to Christ in our effectual calling (Ephesians 3:17; 1 Corinthians 1:9).

34. Q. What is effectual calling?

A. Effectual calling is the work of God's Spirit (2 Timothy 1:9; 2 Thessalonians 2:13-14), whereby convincing us of our sin and misery (Acts 2:37), enlightening our minds in the knowledge of Christ (Acts 26:18), and renewing our wills (Ezekiel 36:26-27), He doth persuade and enable us to embrace Jesus Christ freely offered to us in the gospel (John 6:44-45; Philippians 2:13).

35. Q. What benefits do they who are effectually called partake of in this life?

A. They who are effectually called in this life do partake of justification (Romans 8:30), adoption (Ephesians 1:5), sanctification, and the several benefits which in this life do either accompany or flow from them (1 Corinthians 1:30).

36. Q. What is justification?

A. Justification is an act of God's free grace, wherein He pardons all our sins (Romans 3:24-25; 4:6-8) and accepts us as righteous in His sight (2 Corinthians 5:19, 21) only by the righteousness of Christ imputed to us (Romans 5:17-19), and is received by faith alone (Galatians 2:16; Philippians 3:9).

37. Q. What is adoption?

A. Adoption is an act of God's free grace (1 John 3:1), whereby we are received into the number and have a right to all the privileges of the sons of God (John 1:12; Romans 8:14-17).

38. Q. What is sanctification?

A. Sanctification is the work of God's free grace (2 Thessalonians 2:13), whereby we are renewed in the whole man after the image of God (Ephesians 4:23-24) and are enabled more and more to die unto sin and live unto righteousness (Romans 6:4, 6; 8:1).

39. Q. What are the benefits in this life that accompany or flow from justification, adoption, and sanctification?

A. The benefits in this life that accompany or flow from justification, adoption, and sanctification are assurance of God's love, peace of conscience (Romans 5:1, 2, 5), joy in the Holy Spirit (Romans 5:5, 17), increase of grace (Proverbs 4:18), and perseverance therein to the end (1 John 5:13; 1 Peter 1:5).

40. Q. What benefits do believers receive from Christ at their death?

A. The souls of believers are, at their death, made perfect in holiness (Hebrews 12:23) and do immediately pass into glory (2 Corinthians 5:1, 6, 8; Philippians 1:23; Luke 23:43); and their bodies, being still united to Christ (1 Thessalonians 4:14), do rest in their graves (Isaiah 57:2) till the resurrection (Job 19:26-27).

41. Q. What benefits do believers receive from Christ at the resurrection?

A. At the resurrection, believers, being raised up in glory (1 Corinthians 15:43), shall be openly acknowledged and acquitted in the day of judgment (Matthew 25:23; 10:32) and made perfectly blessed, both in soul and body, in the full enjoyment of God (1 John 3:2; 1 Corinthians 13:12) to all eternity (1 Thessalonians 4:17-18).

42. Q. But what shall be done to the wicked at their death?

A. The souls of the wicked shall, at their death, be cast into the torments of Hell, and their bodies lie in their graves till the resurrection and judgment of the great day (Luke 16:23-24; Acts 2:24; Jude 5, 7; 1 Peter 3:19; Psalm 49:14).

43. Q. What shall be done to the wicked at their day of judgment?

A. At their day of judgment, the bodies of the wicked, being raised out of their graves, shall be sentenced, together with their souls, to unspeakable torments with the devil and his angels forever (John 5:28-29; Matthew 25:41, 46; 2 Thessalonians 1:8-9).

44. Q. What is the duty which God requires of man?

A. The duty which God requires of man is obedience to His revealed will (Micah 6:8; 1 Samuel 15:22).

45. Q. What did God at first reveal to man for the rule of his obedience?

A. The rule which God at first revealed to man for his obedience was the law written on his heart (Romans 2:14-15).

46. Q. What law did God give to Israel under the Old Covenant?

A. The law which God gave to Israel under the Old Covenant is summarily comprehended in the Ten Commandments (Deuteronomy 10:4; Matthew 19:17).

47. Q. On what two commandments hang all the Law and the Prophets?

A. All the Law and the Prophets hang on these commandments: to "'love the Lord your God with all your heart, with all your soul, with all your strength, and with all your mind'" and "'to love your neighbor as yourself'" (Matthew 22:37-39).

48. Q. What is the preface to the Ten Commandments?

A. The preface to the Ten Commandments is in these words: "I am the LORD thy God, which have brought thee out of the land of Egypt, out of the house of bondage" (Exodus 20:2).

49. Q. What can we learn from the preface to the Ten Commandments?

A. The preface to the Ten Commandments teaches us that because God is the Lord, and our God and Redeemer, therefore, we are bound to obey His will (Luke 1:74-75; 1 Peter 1:15-19).

50. Q. Which is the first commandment?

A. The first commandment is, "Thou shalt have no other gods before me" (Exodus 20:3).

51. Q. What can we learn from the first commandment?

A. The first commandment teaches us to know and acknowledge God to be the only true God and our God (1 Chronicles 28:9; Deuteronomy 26:17) and to worship and glorify Him accordingly (Matthew 4:10; Psalm 29:2).

52. Q. What else can we learn from the first commandment?

A. The first commandment also shows us the sinfulness of denying (Psalm 14:1) or not worshipping and glorifying the true God as God and our God (Psalm 81:10, 11; Romans 1:21), and the giving of that worship and glory to any other, which is due unto Him alone (Romans 1:25-26).

53. Q. What are we especially taught by the words "before me" in the first commandment?

A. The words "before me" in the first commandment teach us that God, Who sees all things, takes notice of and is much displeased with the sin of having any other god (Exodus 8:5-32).

54. Q. Which is the second commandment?

A. The second commandment is, "Thou shalt not make unto thee any graven image, or any likeness of anything that is in heaven above, or that is in the earth beneath, or that is in the water under the earth. Thou shalt not bow down thyself to them, nor serve them: for I the Lord thy God am a jealous God, visiting the iniquity of the fathers upon the children unto the third and fourth generation of them that hate me; And showing mercy unto thousands of them that love me, and keep my commandments" (Exodus 20:4-6).

55. Q. What can we learn from the second commandment?

A. The second commandment teaches us that we must receive, observe, and keep pure and entire all such religious worship and ordinances as God has appointed in His word (Deuteronomy 32:46; Matthew 23:20; Acts 2:42).

56. Q. What else can we learn from the second commandment?

A. The second commandment also shows us the sinfulness of worshipping God by images (Deuteronomy 4:15-19; Exodus 32:5, 8), or any other way not appointed in His Word (Deuteronomy 7:31-32).

57. Q. What are the reasons annexed to the second commandment?

A. The reasons annexed to the second commandment are God's sovereignty over us (Psalm 45:2-3, 6), His propriety in us (Psalm 45:11), and the zeal He hath to His own worship (Exodus 34:13-14).

58. Q. Which is the third commandment?

A. The third commandment is, "Thou shalt not take the name of the Lord thy God in vain; for the Lord will not hold him guiltless that taketh his name in vain" (Exodus 20:7).

59. Q. What can we learn from the third commandment?

A. The third commandment teaches us to make holy and reverent use of God's names (Matthew 6:9; Deuteronomy 23:58), titles (Psalm 68:4), attributes (Revelation 15:3-4), ordinances (Malachi 1:11, 14), Word (Psalm 136:1-2) and works (Job 36:24).

60. Q. What else can we learn from the third commandment?

A. The third commandment also shows us the sinfulness of profaning and abusing anything whereby God makes Himself known (Malachi 1:6-7, 12; 2:2; 3:14)

61. Q. What is the reason annexed to the third commandment?

A. The reason annexed to the third commandment is that however the breakers of this commandment may escape punishment from men, yet the Lord our God will not suffer them to escape His righteous judgment (1 Samuel 2:12, 17, 22, 29; 3:13; Deuteronomy 28:58-59).

62. Q. What is the fourth commandment?

A. The fourth commandment is, "Remember the sabbath day, to keep it holy. Six days shalt thou labor, and do all thy work: But the seventh day is the sabbath of the LORD thy God: in it thou shalt not do any work, thou, nor thy son, nor thy daughter, thy manservant, nor thy maidservant, nor thy cattle, nor thy stranger that is within thy gates: For in six days the Lord made heaven and earth, the sea, and all that in them is, and rested the seventh day: wherefore the Lord blessed the sabbath day, and hallowed it" (Exodus 20:8-11).

63. Q. What can we learn from the fourth commandment?

A. The fourth commandment teaches us to keep holy to God such set times as He hath appointed in His Word (Exodus 20:8-11; Deuteronomy 5:12-14).

64. Q. Which day hath God appointed to be our day of worship?

A. Before the resurrection of Christ, God appointed the seventh day of the week to be the weekly Sabbath (Exodus 20:8-11; Deuteronomy 5:12-14); but under the New Covenant, the first day of the week is the Lord's Day and the proper day for worship (Psalm 118:24; Matthew 28:1; Mark 2:27-28; John 20:19-20, 26; Revelation 1:10; Mark 16:2; Luke 24:1; 30-36; John 20:1; Acts 1:3; 2:1-2; 20:7; 1 Corinthians 16:1-2).

65. Q. How is the Lord's Day to be sanctified?

A. The Lord's Day is sanctified by spending the day in the public and private exercises of God's worship (Acts 20:7).

66. Q. What is forbidden on the Lord's Day?

A. The omission or careless performance of the duties required and profaning the day by idleness (Acts 20:7, 9) or doing that which is in itself sinful are forbidden on the Lord's Day.

67. Q. What are the reasons annexed to the fourth commandment?

A. The reasons annexed to the fourth commandment are God's allowing six days of the week for lawful employment (Exodus 20:9), His challenging a special propriety in a seventh day, His own example, and His blessing on the seventh day (Exodus 20:11).

68. Q. Which is the fifth commandment?

A. The fifth commandment is, "Honour thy father and thy mother: that thy days may be long upon the land which the LORD thy God giveth thee" (Exodus 20:12).

69. Q. What can we learn from the fifth commandment?

A. The fifth commandment teaches us to preserve the honor and perform the duties belonging to everyone in their several places and relations, as superiors (Ephesians 5:21), inferiors (1 Peter 2:17), or equals (Romans 12:10).

70. Q. What else can we learn from the fifth commandment?

A. The fifth commandment also shows us the sinfulness of the neglect, or doing anything against, the honor and duty which belongs to everyone in their several places and relations (Matthew 15:4-6; Ezekiel 34:24; Romans 13:8).

71. Q. What is the reason annexed to the fifth commandment?

A. The reason annexed to the fifth commandment is a promise of long life and prosperity (as far as it shall serve for God's glory and their own good) to all such as keep this commandment (Deuteronomy 5:16; Ephesians 6:2-3).

72. Q. What is the sixth commandment?

A. The sixth commandment is, "Thou shalt not kill" (Exodus 20:13).

73. Q. What can we learn from the sixth commandment?

A. The sixth commandment teaches us to make all lawful endeavors to preserve our own life (Ephesians 5:28-29) and the life of others (1 Kings 18:4).

74. Q. What else can we learn from the sixth commandment?

A. The sixth commandment also shows us the absolute sinfulness of taking away our own life, or the life of our neighbor unjustly, or whatsoever tends thereunto (Acts 26:28; Genesis 9:9).

75. Q. Which is the seventh commandment?

A. The seventh commandment is, "Thou shalt not commit adultery" (Exodus 20:14).

76. Q. What can we learn from the seventh commandment?

A. The seventh commandment teaches us to preserve our own and our neighbors' chastity in heart, speech, and behavior (1 Corinthians 7:2-3, 5, 34, 36; Colossians 4:6; 1 Peter 3:2).

77. Q. What else can we learn from the seventh commandment?

A. The seventh commandment also shows us the sinfulness of all unchaste thoughts, words, and actions (Matthew 15:19; 5:28; Ephesians 5:3-4).

78. Q. Which is the eighth commandment?

A. The eighth commandment is, "Thou shalt not steal" (Exodus 20:15).

79. Q. What can we learn from the eighth commandment?

A. The eighth commandment teaches us to lawfully procure and further the wealth and outward estate of ourselves and others (Genesis 30:30; 1 Timothy 5:8; Leviticus 25:35; Deuteronomy 22:1-5; Exodus 23:4-5; Genesis 47:14, 20).

80. Q. What else can we learn from the eighth commandment?

A. The eighth commandment also shows us the sinfulness of whatsoever doth or may unjustly hinder our own (1 Timothy 5:8; Proverbs 28:19) or our neighbor's wealth or outward estate (Proverbs 21:17; 23:20-21; Ephesians 4:28).

81. Q. Which is the ninth commandment?

A. The ninth commandment is, "Thou shalt not bear false witness against thy neighbour" (Exodus 20:16).

82. Q. What can we learn from the ninth commandment?

A. The ninth commandment teaches us to maintain and promote truth between us and man (Zechariah 8:16), and of our neighbor's good name (John 5:12), especially in witness bearing (Proverbs 14:5, 25).

83. Q. What else can we learn from the ninth commandment?

A. The ninth commandment also shows us the sinfulness of whatsoever is prejudicial to the truth or injurious to our own or our neighbor's good name (1 Samuel 17:28; Leviticus 19:16; Psalm 15:2-3).

84. Q. Which is the tenth commandment?

A. The tenth commandment is, "Thou shalt not covet thy neighbor's house, thou shalt not covet thy neighbour's wife, nor his manservant, nor his maidservant, nor his ox, nor his ass, nor anything that is thy neighbour's" (Exodus 20:17).

85. Q. What can we learn from the tenth commandment?

A. The tenth commandment teaches us to have full contentment with our own condition (Hebrews 13:5; 1 Timothy 6:6), with a right and charitable frame of spirit toward our neighbor and all that is his (Job 31:29; Romans 7:15; 1 Timothy 1:5; 1 Corinthians 8:4, 7).

86. Q. What else can we learn from the tenth commandment?

A. The tenth commandment also shows us the sinfulness of all discontentment with our own estate (1 Kings 21:4; Esther 5:13; 1 Corinthians 10:10), envying or grieving at the good of our neighbor (Galatians 5:26; James 3:14, 16), and all inordinate motions and affections to anything that is theirs (Romans 7:7-8; 13:9; Deuteronomy 5:21).

87. Q. Is any man able to perfectly keep the commandments of God?

A. No mere man since the Fall is able in this life to perfectly keep the commandments of God (Ecclesiastes 7:20; 1 John 1:8, 10; Galatians 5:17), but doth daily break them in thought, word, or deed (Genesis 4:5; 7:21; Romans 3:9-21; James 3:2-13).

88. Q. Are all transgressions equally heinous?

A. Some sins in themselves, and by reason of several aggravations, are more heinous in the sight of God than others (Ezekiel 8:6, 13, 15; 1 John 5:16; Psalm 78:17, 32, 56).

89. Q. What doth every sin deserve?

A. Every sin deserves God's wrath and curse, both in this life and that which is to come (Ephesians 5:6; Galatians 3:10; Lamentations 3:39; Matthew 25:41; Romans 6:23).

90. Q. What doth God require of us that we may escape His wrath and curse due to us for sin?

A. To escape the wrath and curse of God due to us for sin, God requires of us faith in Jesus Christ and repentance unto life (Acts 20:21) with the diligent use of all the outward means, whereby Christ communicates to us the benefits of redemption (Proverbs 2:1-6, 8:33-36; Isaiah 55:2-3).

91. Q. What is faith in Jesus Christ?

A. Faith in Jesus Christ is a saving grace (Hebrews 10:39), whereby we receive and rest upon Him alone for salvation, as He is offered to us in the gospels (John 1:12; Isaiah 26:3, 4; Philippians 3:9; Galatians 2:16).

92. Q. What is repentance unto life?

A. Repentance unto life is a saving grace (Acts 11:28), whereby a sinner, out of a true sense of his sin (Acts 2:37-38) and apprehension of the mercy of God in Christ (Joel 2:12; Jeremiah 3:22) doth, with grief and hatred of his sin, turn from it unto God (Jeremiah 31:18-19; Ezekiel 36:31), with full purpose of and endeavor after new obedience (2 Corinthians 7:11; Isaiah 1:16-17).

93. Q. What are the outward means whereby Christ communicates to us the benefits of redemption?

A. The outward and ordinary means whereby Christ communicates to us the benefits of redemption are His ordinances, especially the Word, baptism, the Lord's Supper, and prayer (Matthew 28:19-20; Acts 2:42, 46-47).

94. Q. How is the Word made effectual to salvation and spiritual growth?

A. The Spirit of God makes the reading, but especially the preaching, of the Word an effectual means of convincing and converting sinners and of building them up in holiness and comfort through faith unto salvation (Nehemiah 8:8; Acts 26:18; Psalm 19:8; Acts 20:32; Romans 1:15-16; 10:13-17, 15:4; 1 Corinthians 14:24-25; 1 Timothy 3:15-17).

95. Q. How is the Word to be read and heard that it may become an effectual means of spiritual growth?

A. That the Word may become effectual for our spiritual growth, we must attend thereunto with diligence (Proverbs 8:34) and prayer (Psalm 119:18), receive it with faith and love (Hebrews 4:2; 2 Thessalonians 2:10), lay it up in our hearts (Psalm 119:18), and practice it in our lives (Luke 8:15; James 1:25).

96. Q. How do baptism and the Lord's Supper become effectual means of spiritual growth?

A. Baptism and the Lord's Supper become effectual means of spiritual growth, not for any virtue in them, or in those who doth administer them, but only by the blessing of Christ (1 Peter 3:21; Matthew 3:11; 1 Corinthians 3:6-7) and the working of the Spirit in those who by faith receive them (1 Corinthians 12:3; Matthew 28:19).

97. Q. What is baptism?

A. Baptism is an ordinance of the New Testament instituted by Jesus Christ to be unto the party baptized a sign of their fellowship with Him in His death, burial, and resurrection; of his being ingrafted into Him (Romans 6:3-5; Colossians 2:12; Galatians 3:27); of remission of sins (Mark 1:4; Acts 2:38; 22:16); and of them giving up themselves unto God through Jesus Christ to live and walk in newness of life (Romans 6:3-4).

98. Q. To whom is baptism to be administered?

A. Baptism is to be administered to all those who actually profess repentance toward God (Acts 2:38; Matthew 3:6), faith in and obedience to our Lord Jesus Christ, and to none other (Acts 8:12, 36-38; 10:47-48).

99. Q. Are the infants of professing believers to be baptized?

A. The infants of professing believers are not to be baptized because there is neither command or example or certain consequence from the holy Scriptures to baptize such (Exodus 23:13; Proverbs 30:6; Luke 3:7-8).

100. Q. How is baptism rightly administered?

A. Baptism is rightly administered by immersion, or dipping the whole body of the party in water, in the name of the Father, and of the Son, and of the Holy Spirit, according to Christ's institution and the practice of the apostles (Matthew 3:16; John 3:23; 4:1-2; Matthew 28:19-20; Acts 8:38; Romans 6:4; Colossians 2:12), and not by sprinkling or pouring of water, or dipping some part of the body after the tradition of men.

101. Q. What is the duty of such who are rightly baptized?

A. It is the duty of such who are rightly baptized to give up themselves to some particular and orderly church of Jesus Christ, that they may walk in all the commandments and ordinances of the Lord blameless (Acts 2:41-42; 5:13-14; 9:26; 1 Peter 2:5; Luke 1:6).

102. Q. What is the Lord's Supper?

A. The Lord's Supper is an ordinance of the New Testament instituted by Jesus Christ, wherein by giving and receiving bread and wine, according to His appointment, His death is shown forth, and the worthy receivers are, not after a corporal and carnal manner, but by faith, made partakers of His body and blood, with all His benefits, to their spiritual nourishment and growth in grace (Matthew 26:26-28; 1 Corinthians 11:23-26; 10:16).

103. Q. Who are the proper subjects of this ordinance?

A. They who have been baptized upon a personal profession of their faith in Jesus Christ and repentance from dead works are the proper subjects of this ordinance (Acts 2:41-42).

104. Q. What is required for the worthy receiving of the Lord's Supper?

A. It is required of them who would worthily partake of the Lord's Supper that they examine themselves of their knowledge to discern the Lord's body (1 Corinthians 11:28-29), of their faith to feed upon Him (2 Corinthians 13:5), of their repentance (1 Corinthians 11:31), of their love (1 Corinthians 10:16-17), and of their new obedience (1 Corinthians 5:7-8), lest coming unworthily they eat and drink judgment to themselves (1 Corinthians 11:28-29).

105. Q. What is prayer?

A. Prayer is offering up our desires to God (Psalm 62:8) by the assistance of the Holy Spirit (Romans 8:26) for things agreeable to His will (1 John 5:14; Romans 8:27) in the name of Christ (John 16:23), believing (Matthew 21:22; James 1:6) with confession of our sins (Psalm 32:5-6; Daniel 9:4) and thankful acknowledgment of His mercies (Philippians 4:6).

106. Q. What rule hath God given for our direction in prayer?

A. The whole Word of God is of use to direct us in prayer (1 John 5:14), but the special rule of direction is the prayer which Christ taught His disciples, commonly called the Lord's Prayer (Matthew 6:9-13; Luke 11:2-4).

107. Q. What doth the preface of the Lord's Prayer teach us?

A. The preface of the Lord's Prayer, which is, "Our Father which art in heaven" (Matthew 6:9) teaches us to draw near to God with all holy reverence and confidence as children to a Father able and ready to help us (Romans 8:15; Luke 11:13; Isaiah 24:8) and that we should pray with and for others (Acts 12:5; 1 Timothy 2:1-2).

108. Q. What do we pray for in the first petition?

A. In the first petition, which is, "Hallowed be thy name" (Matthew 6:9), we pray that God would enable us and others to glorify Him in all that He makes Himself known (Psalm 67:2-3) and that He would dispose all things to His own glory (Psalm 83; Romans 11:36).

109. Q. What do we pray for in the second petition?

A. In the second petition, which is, "Thy kingdom come" (Matthew 6:10), we pray that

Satan's kingdom may be destroyed (Psalm 68:1, 18) and that the grace of God may be advanced (Revelation 12:10-11), ourselves and others brought into it and kept in it (2 Thessalonians 3:1; Romans 10:1; John 17:19-20), and that the kingdom of glory may be hastened (Revelation 22:10).

110. Q. What do we pray for in the third petition?

A. In the third petition, which is, "Thy will be done in earth, as it is in heaven" (Matthew 6:10), we pray that God by His grace would make us able and willing to know, obey, and submit to His will in all things (Psalm 67; 119:36; 2 Samuel 15:25; Job 1:21), as the angels do in Heaven (Psalm 103:20-21).

111. Q. What do we pray for in the fourth petition?

A. In the fourth petition, which is, "Give us this day our daily bread" (Matthew 6:11), we pray that of God's free gift we may receive a competent portion of the good things of this life and enjoy His blessing with them (Proverbs 30:8; Genesis 28:20; 1 Timothy 4:4-5).

112. Q. What do we pray for in the fifth petition?

A. In the fifth petition, which is, "And forgive us our debts, as we forgive our debtors" (Matthew 6:12), we pray that God, for Christ's sake, would freely pardon all our sins (Psalm 51:1-2, 7, 9; Daniel 9:17-19), which we are rather encouraged to ask because of His grace by which we are enabled from the heart to forgive others (Luke 11:4; Matthew 18:35).

113. Q. What do we pray for in the sixth petition?

A. In the sixth petition, which is, "And lead us not into temptation, but deliver us from evil" (Matthew 6:13), we pray that God would either keep us from being tempted to sin (Matthew 26:31) or support and deliver us when we are tempted (2 Corinthians 12:8).

114. Q. What doth the conclusion of the Lord's Prayer teach?

A. The conclusion of the Lord's Prayer, which is, "For Thine is the kingdom, and the power, and the glory, for ever, Amen" (Matthew 6:13), teaches us to take our encouragement in prayer from God only (Daniel 9:4, 7-9, 16-19), and in our prayers to praise Him, ascribing kingdom, power, and glory to Him (1 Chronicles 29:10-13). And in testimony of our desire and assurance of being heard, we say, Amen (1 Corinthians 4:16; Revelation 11:20; 22:20-21).

ABOUT THE EDITOR

Brandon James Crawford (Ph.D. in historical theology [Cand.], Puritan Reformed Theological Seminary) is the senior pastor of Grace Baptist Church in Marshall, Michigan; the moderator of the Southern Michigan Association of Regular Baptist Churches; and a Council of Sixteen member in the Michigan Association of Regular Baptist Churches. He has written or contributed to a number of books on historical theology, including *The Jonathan Edwards Encyclopedia* (Eerdmans), *Petrus van Mastricht (1630-1706): Text, Context, and Interpretation* (Vandenhoeck & Ruprecht), *The Miscellanies Companion* vols. 1 and 2 (JESociety Press), and *Jonathan Edwards on the Atonement* (Wipf and Stock). He and his wife, Melanie, have two children.

Ambassador International's mission is to magnify the Lord Jesus Christ and promote His gospel through the written word.

We believe through the publication of Christian literature, Jesus Christ and His Word will be exalted, believers will be strengthened in their walk with Him, and the lost will be directed to Jesus Christ as the only way of salvation.

For more information about
AMBASSADOR INTERNATIONAL
please connect at:

www.ambassador-international.com

If you enjoyed this book, please consider leaving us a review on Amazon, Goodreads, or our website.